Study Guide

Rosalind Gottfried, Ph.D

SEVENTH EDITION

Social Problems

William Kornblum
Graduate School and University Center
City University of New York

Joseph Julian
San Francisco State University

In collaboration with
Carolyn D. Smith

Prentice Hall, Englewood Cliffs, New Jersey 07632

Production Editor: *Kris Ann E. Cappelluti*
Acquisitions Editor: *Nancy Roberts*
Supplements Acquisitions Editor: *Sharon Chambliss*
Pre-press Buyer: *Kelly Behr*
Manufacturing Buyer: *Mary Ann Gloriande*

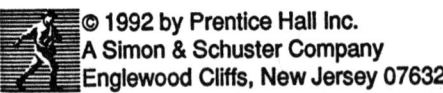
© 1992 by Prentice Hall Inc.
A Simon & Schuster Company
Englewood Cliffs, New Jersey 07632

All rights reserved. No part of this book may be
reproduced, in any form or by any means,
without permission in writing from the publisher.

Printed in the United States of America

10 9 8 7 6 5 4 3

ISBN 0-13-816273-5

Prentice-Hall International (UK) Limited, *London*
Prentice-Hall of Australia Pty. Limited, *Sydney*
Prentice-Hall Canada Inc. *Toronto*
Prentice-Hall Hispanoamericana, S.A., *Mexico*
Prentice-Hall of India Private Limited, *New Delhi*
Prentice-Hall of Japan, Inc., *Tokyo*
Simon & Schuster Asia Pte. Ltd., *Singapore*
Editora Prentice-Hall do Brasil, Ltda., *Rio de Janeiro*

CONTENTS

	Page
Preface	v
Chapter 1: Socialogical Perspectives on Social Problems	1
Chapter 2: Problems of Physical Health	8
Chapter 3: Mental Illness	16
Chapter 4: Sex-Related Social Problems	23
Chapter 5: Alcohol and Other Drugs	30
Chapter 6: Crime and Criminals	38
Chapter 7: Violence	46
Chapter 8: Poverty Amid Affluence.	53
Chapter 9: Prejucice and Discrimination	61
Chapter 10: Sex Roles and Inequality	69
Chapter 11: An Aging Society	76
Chapter 12: The Changing Family.	83
Chapter 13: Problems of Public Education	89
Chapter 14: Corporations, Workers, and Consumers .	95
Chapter 15: Urban Problems	102
Chapter 16: Population and Immigration	108
Chapter 17: Technology and the Environmental . . .	113
Chapter 18: War and Terrorism.	118

PREFACE

This Study Guide is designed to help the student absorb the information in this text. It is organized to facilitate an understanding of the theories and analysis in the text and not simply to aid the student in memorizing relevant information. Each chapter begins with a broadly based set of learning objectives which inform the student of the basic knowledge she or he should have after studying the text. A brief chapter summary outlines these objectives in narrative form.

Each chapter then offers a detailed outline of the textbook chapters which summarizes the material in the text. Key terms follow the outline to highlight terminology and/or concepts new to the student.

Practice tests with multiple choice questions and essay questions are next. Answers are provided to both sets of questions. The answers provided for the essays point to some of the relevant issues suggested by the questions. The essay questions are also meant to promote thought beyond the material printed in the text.

We hope that you find this study guide useful in your learning experience.

CHAPTER ONE: SOCIOLOGICAL PERSPECTIVES ON SOCIAL PROBLEMS

Chapter Summary:

The chapter begins with a consideration of what constitutes a social problem. Major sociological perspectives on social problems are reviewed. These include the functionalist, conflict, and interactionist perspectives. Each contains a different view of how social problems are defined and how they should be addressed.

Sociologists hold many assumptions which influence their studies of social problems. These include different conceptions of the same behaviors over time; differing views of behaviors in terms of who is exhibiting them; a variety of views on how things should be changed. All of these views are effected by a person's status in society.

Researchers examine problems through a variety of research methods. These include demographic studies, survey methods, fieldwork, and experiments. This research helps social scientists, politicians, and others formulate the social policies developed to address social problems. The chapter ends with a summary of social policy trends.

Learning Objectives:

After studying the chapter the student should be able:
- to elaborate the nature of what is considered to be a social problem. Provide examples of issues considered to be social problems.
- to explain the three major perspectives in sociological theory -- functionalist, conflict, interactionist -- and describe how each views the cause and treatment of social problems.
- to understand that different things are perceived as social problems depending on one's point of view. To understand the assumptions sociologists hold in dealing with the area of social problems.
- to be able to identify the nature and function of the different research methods.
- to explain what social policy is and what the liberal and conservative views of policy typically contain.

Chapter Outline:
I. What is a Social Problem?
    A. Most generally any condition that threatens major values or the quality of life. Usually there is a broad consensus on these. The issue is usually considered a problem for the entire society.
        1. Easily identifiable examples: crime, drug abuse, poverty, juvenile delinquency.
        2. Other examples: sexism, racism, ageism, violence, drunken driving, unemployment.

B. What constitutes a social problem changes over time. The lack of voting rights was not generally considered a problem until the suffragettes publicized it.
II. Sociological Perspectives on Social Problems
 A. The functionalist perspective focuses on the ways major institutions operate. Major institutions are assumed to fulfill particular functions to create a working whole. Social problems occur when a major institution is failing to perform its function. Such failure is generally seen to result from social changes in society.
  1. Institutions that were functional in the past may not be so today. This could be due to changes in social conditions and/or values.
  2. This perspective views problems as social pathologies. This is because society is viewed as an organic whole. Anything that is wrong in the organism is seen to be an illness. This view is not widely held today.
  3. The social disorganization view looks at what happens when social expectations or rules fail.
III. The Conflict Perspective
 A. Problems stem from contradictions in the organization of society. Some people are the "haves" and others the "have nots." Problems stem from conflicts between these groups.
  1. The perspective stems from the work of Karl Marx. He viewed society in terms of the different needs of the workers and the owners of production. This class conflict was seen to be a consequence of capitalist society. Social problems stemmed from the concentration of wealth and power in the hands of a few people.
  2. Value Conflict Theory: views social problems in terms of conditions incompatible with group values.
IV. The Interactionist Perspective
 A. Unlike the previous two theories, this theory views the process by which an individual becomes part of a situation defined as a problem. People are often greatly influenced by whatever group they define as their peer group.
  1. The labeling theory suggests that it is the reaction of society, rather than the behavior itself, which separates the deviant from the non-deviant.
V. Assumptions About Social Problems
 A. Often what is defined as a social problem stems from unintended consequences of acceptable behaviors. An example would be the result of Prohibition as seen in the rise of organized crime.
 B. The social structure itself causes many to conform but others to deviate. An example of this would be

stealing to fulfill the need to have material goods.
  C. The recognition that people in different social strata will perceive different behaviors as social problems and advance different solutions. Different attitudes towards tax reforms provides an example of this type.
VI. Research on Social Problems
  A. Demographic studies examine the distribution of social conditions in the population.
  B. Survey research utilizes samples representing a population to be studied. These samples may be cross-sectional or longitudinal.
  C. Field observation is the direct observation of social behaviors.
  D. Experiments attempt to systematically control conditions to determine the effects of particular conditions.
VII. Social Policy
  A. Social policies are mechanisms and approaches towards remedying problems. Conservatives tend to want to limit government involvement while liberals want to extend it.

Key Terms:
Social Problems: conditions perceived by societal members to threaten the quality of life and/or major values.
Status: a position in a group or institution.
Role: behavior performed because of status held.
Institution: a more or less stable set of statuses and roles meeting basic needs in society.
Functionalist Perspective: views social problems as the failure of an institution to adapt to social changes.
Social Pathology: the functionalist view sees social problems as illnesses in the organism of society.
Social Disorganization: a functionalist view that looks at what happens when institutional expectations or roles fail.
Conflict Perspective: views social problems as the contradiction between the interests of a small, powerful group and the rest of society.
Value Conflict Theory: a conflict perspective looking at conditions incompatible with group values.
The Interactionist Perspective: views the process by which an individual becomes involved in behaviors or groups defined as social problems.
Labeling Theory: focuses on societal reactions to behaviors rather than the behavior itself, in defining deviance.
Demography: is the statistical study of trends in the population.
Survey Research: collecting information from a group of

people thought to be representative of a larger group.
Longitudinal Survey: studying the same group of people over a period of time.
Cross-sectional Survey: looking at a variety of groups at one period in time.
Social Policies: are formal procedures and ideas concerning the remedy of a social problem.

Practice Test:
Multiple Choice Questions: Select the best answer for each question below.
1. What is the definition of a social problem:
    a. problems interacting with people at a party
    b. problems defined by society as threatening ✓
    c. people who are unhappy with their marriages
    d. none of the above.
2. Which of the following would **NOT** be considered a social problem by society?
    a. crime
    b. drug abuse
    c. the medical profession ✓
    d. juvenile delinquency.
3. Which of the following can be considered a social problem?
    a. a person unhappy in their job ✓
    b. racism ✓
    c. a person who does not vote
    d. none of the above.
4. The functionalist view is interested in all of the following **EXCEPT**:
    a. who has the power ✓
    b. the interaction of major institutions
    c. the major roles in society
    d. what happens to adjust to social changes.
5. The functionalist view:
    a. no longer agrees with the pathology concept ✓
    b. still promotes the idea of social pathology
    c. is not very interested in criminal deviance
    d. is not interested in comparing crime in different countries.
6. The social disorganization view:
    a. is a functionalist view
    b. looks at normlessness
    c. looks at cultural conflict
    d. all of the above. ✓
7. Conflict theory views social problems:
    a. as institutions in need of reform
    b. contradictions between a small group and the rest of society ✓
    c. as unrelated to the place of power in society

8.   d. as unrelated to the capitalist system.
8. Marxian views of crime:
    a. treat street drug use and prescriptive drug use as the same problem
    b. treat upper class and lower class offenders the same way
    c. seek to reform existing institutions
    ⓓ. none of the above.
9. Examples of problems easily viewed in the value conflict perspective include all of the following EXCEPT:
    a. the abortion issue
    b. the pornography issue
    ⓒ. the issue of rape
    d. the issue of marijuana smoking.
10. The Interactionist Theory attributes a lot of influence to the _____ group:
    a. family
    b. sibling
    ⓒ. peer
    d. parent.
11. Labeling Theory suggests:
    a. deviance lies in the act itself
    ⓑ. deviance is in the eye of the beholders
    c. deviance is the same no matter who commits the act
    d. none of the above.
12. Which of the following is an assumption typical of the consideration of social problems:
    a. all deviant acts are considered to be equivalent
    ⓑ. some groups view a behavior as deviant while others do not
    c. rich or poor, everyone has the same program for economic reform
    d. problems are stable over time.
13. The study of full population trends may be seen in:
    ⓐ. demographic research
    b. survey methods
    c. fieldwork
    d. social experiments.
14. A researcher trying to predict who would win the presidential election, if it were this week, would use which research method:
    a. demographic research
    ⓑ. survey methods
    c. fieldwork
    d. social experiments.
15. Becker's famous study of marijuana smokers indicated:
    a. anyone can get high
    b. a high experience is a universal one
    ⓒ. the experience of a high is a socially constructed one

      d. none of the above.
16. The Zimbardo study on prison life indicated:
      a. prison itself had little impact on behavior
      b. students are a bad sample because they don't take anything seriously
      c. that personality characteristics are set early in life
      d. the subjects did treat the experimental conditions as if it were real.
17. Social policies with regard to social problems:
      a. have extended the government's role in this century
      b. are promoted through government participation by conservatives
      c. are reduced in terms of government intervention by liberals
      d. none of the above.

Essay Questions:
Students should address the following issues:
1. Give examples of things that are widely held to be social problems. Give examples of things which are not always seen to be social problems. Explain differences between the two groups.
2. Compare and contrast aspects of the three major views of social problems.
3. Sociologists tend to talk about social problems and deviance together. Why? What is the relationship between the two concepts?
4. What type of social policies should be used to address social problems?

Test Answers:
Multiple Choice Questions:
1. b
2. c
3. b
4. a
5. a
6. d
7. b
8. d
9. c
10. c
11. b
12. b
13. a
14. b
15. c
16. d
17. a

Essay Questions:
Students should address the following issues:
1. The first category would contain things that all people generally view as threatening: crimes, drug abuse, poverty, delinquency.
 - The second category is characterized by things that some people define as problematic while others do not: homosexuality, war, prostitution, pornography, sexism, racism.
 - The latter category depends on one's personal values in the definition of the behaviors as problematic.
2. Which perspective assumes the most social conformity?
 - Which perspective deals best with both social and individual aspects of social problems?
 - Which perspective appears most accurate to your observations?
 - Which view is the most flexible? That is, can it be used to look at many different problems?
3. People who are engaging in behaviors seen as social problems often are considered deviant.
 - This assumes individual guilt for acting in these ways (that are seen as problems).
 - It also assumes a societal consensus in terms of what is considered deviant or problematic.
4. Issues of government intervention and the provision of funding should be included.

CHAPTER TWO: PROBLEMS OF PHYSICAL HEALTH

Chapter Summary:
The chapter opens with a discussion of why health care in the U.S. can be considered a social problem. Major problems in American health care include: unequal access to care; noncomprehensive care; high costs of care; differences in the health care of minorities and women; problems with government programs; the "fee-for-services" approach; lack of preventive health care; the rights and needs of handicapped persons.

Special attention is given to the contemporary problem of the acquired immune deficiency syndrome (AIDS) because of both its threat to the public health and the high cost of caring for its victims. Public and professional debates are focused on both these issues.

The next section of the chapter deals briefly with the ways in which the three major perspectives -- conflict, interactionist, and functionalist -- view problems in the health care industry.

Finally, social policy concerns are addressed. These include ways to change the system and ways to modify parts of the existing system.

Learning Objectives:
After studying the chapter the student should be able:
- to elaborate the reasons contributing to the view of health care as a social problem; to explain why U.S. health care is inferior to other industrial societies.
- to discuss the variety of reasons contributing to the problems in health care in the U.S. including unequal access, high costs of care, economic systems, insurance companies, physician costs, lack of attention and funding for prevention, issues with women's health care, issues concerning the handicapped, and ethical issues.
- to analyze the threat to the public health of the disease AIDS; to understand the facts and myths related to AIDS.
- to be able to explain the viewpoints held by each major sociological perspective on the problems of health care.
- to identify policy issues of concern, in regard to health care, and methods of promoting beneficial reforms in the existing systems.

Chapter Outline:
I. Health Care as a Social Problem
   A. Health care is a large industry. Eight million people are employed in the industry and it accounts for 11% of the Gross National Product.

B. Life expectancy is correlated with the quality of health care. There are large differences between nations, and between social classes in the U.S., in life expectancy.
   1. Health care in the U.S. is inferior to that of other industrial nations. Contributing factors include: number of health care professionals; sedentary occupations; inadequate exercise; environmental pollution and cigarette smoking; unavailability of health care.
C. The U.S. health industry never developed into a competitive market. This was so because: doctors maintain private practices; society supports hospitals and insurance that permit private practice; there are many narrow specialties; special facilities for particular treatments.

II. American Health Care Problems
A. There are micro level, or individual, problems. These include questions of when, or if, to terminate treatments; whether to place an aged parent in an institution. Macro level problems include consideration of the distribution of health care.
B. Health care accessibility is very unequal. About 37 million people have no health insurance and another 20 million have inadequate coverage. Access to health care is not universal.
C. Nonwhites and lower social classes experience lower life expectancies and less health care accessibility.
   1. High rates of infant mortality are associated with socioeconomic status. Problems include: inadequate nutrition, low birth weight, lack of prenatal care, increased incidences of infectious disease.
D. Medicaid has increased the poor's consumption of medical services but not their overall health.
E. Health care costs are largely due to the "fee-for-services" system. The cost of hospital stays, physician fees, unnecessary surgeries, and malpractice insurance contributes to the overall high costs of health care.
F. Inadequate attention to prevention has characterized the American health system. The addition of medicaid and medicare programs has helped but many people are still not covered. The near poor are often not covered by public programs or by private insurance companies.
G. The women's movement has struggled to make the health professionals more sensitive to women's physical and psychological concerns. One aspect of this struggle has been the promotion of alternative practitioners such as midwives.
H. Handicapped persons often are viewed as deviant. Many disabled persons are agitating for mainstreaming

into society rather than for special programs.
   I. Modern medical technology has raised questions concerning the point at which death occurs. Ethical issues have developed concerning the promotion of life-prolonging treatments.
III. AIDS: Acquired Immune Deficiency Syndrome
   A. AIDS is a viral disease with a long period of latency. It has been seen in at least 101 countries. In the U.S., it is found disproportionately among homosexual men, intravenous drug users, blacks, and hispanics.
      1. Health care concerns relating to AIDS include the curtailment of the epidemic, preventive education, research leading to aid and cure for the victims, and greater social awareness of the disease.
IV. Explanations of Health Care Problems
   A. Social class is related to poor health for a number of reasons. Conflict theorists view health care problems in terms of class conflicts.
      1. Many reasons concern conditions of poverty: inadequate diets, polluted areas; occupational hazards; stress; lack of adequate housing.
      2. Other reasons stem from poverty: lack of access to facilities and/or to money to pay for services.
   B. Functionalists view health care problems in terms of failures within the institutions providing health care. Chief among these is the unequal distribution of services. Health care is viewed as a commodity subject to the demands and spending power of the consumer. Critics of this viewpoint believe that health care should not be seen as a commodity.
   C. Interactionist theorists turn their attention to features of the American lifestyle. They point to lack of exercise, poor diet, pollution, and bad habits (e.g., smoking, drinking) as promoting bad health. Their studies focus on patterns of sociability and socialization.
V. Social Policy
   A. Change in the health care system is complicated by competing interests of consumers; labor; minority groups; medical professionals; and the pharmaceutical, health care, and insurance industries. The expansion of the government's role has been implicit in all programs for reform.
   B. Greater focus on prevention is one program for reform. This has especially been promoted by HMOs, prepaid health plans, which have a financial incentive for keeping people healthy.
   C. Some reform measures are geared towards promoting the efficiency of existing health care institutions.

Medicare now pays a flat fee for certain types of procedures.
D. Some programs are geared towards improving existing institutions. Such programs include the expansion of out-patient care, changes in medical education and practices, the advertising of doctor's fees, changes in insurance companies, and training more paraprofessionals.
E. Legislation has been passed (1973, 1975, 1977, 1980, 1983) to help stop discrimination against handicapped persons in all areas of life. Handicapped people are eligible for social security disability payments.
F. Social policy with regard to AIDS brings up serious questions concerning the right of personal privacy and public safety. Policy measures concerning the disease are currently being debated.

Key Terms:
Medicaid: a government program, begun in 1965, to provide health insurance for low-income households.
Fee-for-Services: a system in which a third party covers health care costs to hospitals and doctors.
Medicare: a government program, funded by social security taxes, to cover some of the medical expenses of people over 65 years.
Mainstreaming: integrating special needs groups (disabled, mentally retarded, mentally ill) into the mainstream of life (rather than isolating these groups in special programs).
Living Will: legal documents by patients who are terminally ill (or by healthy people stating desires if they should become so) who do not want their lives prolonged by artificial means.
Mercy Killing: the stopping of life-prolonging treatments.
AIDS: Acquired Immune Deficiency Syndrome -- a disease, identified in at least 101 countries, which is almost always fatal.
Iatrogenic: physician generated, caused by medical treatment (especially in correct doses of medicine).
Health Maintenance Organizations: prepaid group health plans based on a monthly fee.
Handicapped: refers to people who are disfigured, retarded, mentally ill, emotionally disabled, drug or alcohol addicted, suffer from disabling diseases (cancer or heart disease).

Practice Test:
Multiple Choice Questions: Select the best answer for each question below.
1. Which of the following does **NOT** contribute to life

expectancy:
   a. lack of exercise
   b. lack of adequate nutrition
   c. lack of social class differences
   d. lack of health care availability.
2. One problem attributed to the American health system is:
   a. it is not up to modern treatment standards
   b. it is not a competitive industry
   c. standards for medical doctors are loose
   d. there are too many general practitioners.
3. Virtually all Americans have access to adequate health care.
   a. true
   b. false
4. Life expectancy is related to:
   a. social class
   b. race, even controlling for social class
   c. poverty
   d. all of the above.
5. High infant mortality rates are effected by all of the following EXCEPT:
   a. lack of adequate nutrition
   b. poverty
   c. adequate prenatal care
   d. low birth weights.
6. Medicaid has improved the actual health of the poor.
   a. true
   b. false
7. Which of the following has helped to reduce hospital costs:
   a. pre-admission testing on an out-patient basis
   b. the growth of the aged population
   c. insurance companies such as Blue Cross
   d. "fee-for-services" method of payment.
8. What has contributed to the cost of physician's services:
   a. a shortage of physicians
   b. increased specializations
   c. malpractice insurance
   d. all of the above.
9. Many elderly do not receive adequate health care because of all of the following EXCEPT:
   a. they are near-poor and not covered by medicaid
   b. they live in rural areas
   c. they are not eligible for medicare
   d. they cannot pay for deductibles or co-payments.
10. Which of the following is NOT a demand of the women's health movement:
    a. acceptance of midwives
    b. less intervention in the birth process

c. the definition of processes such as menstruation as "illness"
d. the reduction of unnecessary reproductive tract surgeries.
11. Which of the following statements about AIDS is **NOT** true:
a. it is only found in the U.S.
b. it is transmitted only through the exchange of body fluids
c. not every person carrying the virus will develop symptoms
d. there is a latency period of up to five years.
12. AIDS is found disproportionately in which of the following populations:
a. intravenous drug users
b. Blacks
c. homosexual men
d. all of the above.
13. Poor people experience all of the following, with regard to health care, **EXCEPT**:
a. higher rates of illness
b. less access to care
c. less stress
d. adverse conditions stemming from poverty.
14. Which of the following are reasons theorists believe health care should not be seen as a commodity:
a. consumers can't judge the effectiveness of treatments
b. a patient does not have direct control over her or his treatment
c. the number of practitioners is severely restricted
d. all of the above.
15. Which of the following sociological perspectives would be most likely to look at health problems in terms of lifestyle:
a. interactionist
b. Marxian
c. values conflict
d. functionalist
16. Which of the following is **NOT** true with respect to HMOs:
a. they are funded solely by members fees
b. they were promoted by a legislative measure in 1973
c. they have decreased rates of hospitalizations
d. they have clearly reduced overall health costs.
17. Which of the following suggestions have been advanced to improve existing health care institutions:
a. expand out-patient facilities
b. train M.D.s to be general practitioners
c. permit advertising for medical services
d. all of the above.

Essay Questions:
1. Why should the health care system be viewed in terms of a social problem perspective? Explain.
2. What kinds of ethical issues are brought about by medical technology? What are your personal views?
3. Why has AIDS been such an important focal point of concern?
4. Where do you most see the need for change in the provision of health care?

Test Answers:
Multiple Choice:
1. c
2. b
3. b
4. d
5. c
6. b
7. a
8. d
9. c
10. c
11. a
12. d
13. c
14. d
15. a
16. d
17. d

Essay Questions:
The answers should address the following issues:
1. The high rate of infant mortality in the U.S. compared to other industrial nations.
   - the social class differences in health and health care accessibility.
   - the varied health of different races and sexes.
   - the lack of competitive markets in the health industry.
2. Issues of life prolonging interventions for the terminally ill should be addressed. Included would be issues of mercy killing, living wills, prolongation of the life of infants who will not live long.
   - abortion is an issue that remains controversial, in spite of the 1973 Supreme Court decision upholding a woman's right to choose.
3. The threat of an uncontrolled epidemic.
   - the fear of the means of spreading the virus (many do not appear to understand it must be through the exchange of body fluids).
   - the high cost of medical expenses for victims and the related issue of who will pay the bill.
4. Can include any of the following:
   - more nonphysician practitioners
   - more ambulatory (noninstitutional care) home care
   - competitive pricing
   - more HMOs
   - more coverage for all citizens
   - socialized medicine.

CHAPTER THREE: MENTAL ILLNESS

Chapter Summary:

The chapter begins by establishing mental illness as a social problem in terms of the problems individuals experience and in the cost the society undergoes for treatment and social services. Various conceptions of mental illness are examined, especially medical models of illness and sociological perspectives focusing on the social construction and labeling of the mentally ill. Difficulties with classifying mental illness are discussed in relation to the views of mental illness implicit in the major models.

Social conditions such as poverty and urban lifestyles influence mental illness and need to be considered in the development of treatment modalities. Mental hospitals are rarely seen today as the preferred site for treatment. The 1960s was an era which established community based treatment of the mentally ill. Such plans fell short of expectations for these centers. The chapter ends with a discussion of social policy impact on treatment problems for the mentally ill population.

Learning Objectives:

After studying the chapter, the student should be able:
- to explain why the problem of mental illness is considered a social problem
- to explain the "social construction" of mental illness and its relation to normative concepts of behavior
- to understand the theory and practice in the medical model versus nonmedical models of mental illness
- to be able to explain the classification process as a product of the medical model and opposing theories of labeling adhered to by nonmedical theories
- to examine the relationship between social class and the presence and type of mental illness
- to delineate treatment modalities such as hospitalization and community mental health; to refer to issues of medication and funding in relation to these.

Chapter Outline:

I. Mental Illness as a Social Problem
   A. Problems stem from the numbers of people affected by mental illness and through trains in social institutions which attempt to address the problem.
   B. Extreme forms of mental illness can threaten the social order. Such examples represent violent and/or irrational behaviors.
      1. Problems associated with severe mental illness include: family life stress, moral and ethical

problems, social stigmas.
   C. Deinstitutionalization has developed as a social problem in that discharged hospital patients often do not receive adequate support services.
II. The Social Construction of Mental Illness
   A. This view holds that mental illness is derived from social views of "normal" and "deviant."
III. Competing Models of Mental Illness
   A. The medical model is the most established. Mental disorders are considered problems in the personality analogous to physical disturbances in physical diseases.
      1. There is growing evidence that much of severe mental illness is biologically based.
   B. The deviance model of mental illness views mental disorders as departures from social expectations.
      1. Scheff's concept of residual deviance maintains that mental disorders result from people failing to conform to taken-for-granted areas of behavior.
   C. Problems in Living viewpoint sees mental illness largely as a myth. Individuals are not defined as ill but as having unresolved problems in living.
IV. The Classification of Mental Illnesses
   A. Largely the domain of psychiatrists and as standardized in the published volume: The Diagnostic and Statistical Manual of Mental Disorders (DSMIII), published in 1980 and revised in 1987 (DSMIII-R).
      1. The manual represents the medical model.
   B. Is mental illness diagnosed by specific symptoms or labeled as a consequence of violating norms?
      1. Societal factors influence the labeling process.
      2. Research indicates that the diagnosis of mental illness does not accurately separate people into categories of "ill" and "healthy." The label affects perceptions of people's behavior.
V. Inequality, Conflict, and Mental Illness
   A. Poverty and lack of access to adequate treatment are important elements of consideration in the area of social problems. The highest rates of mental disorders are found in inner cities. The lowest rates are found in stable, residential areas with a high socioeconomic status.
      1. Whether mental illness is caused by inner city life or whether the ill drift there is not completely clear.
      2. Studies indicate that random populations will include people with symptoms of mental illness who are not receiving treatment.
   B. Urban life, especially in lower class areas, promotes high levels of stress.
      1. Stresses of poverty and crowding in the home,

contribute to illness.
    C. Race and sex are ascribed characteristics related to incidences and diagnosis of mental disorders. This includes the consequences of discrimination and role expectations in society.
VI. Institutional Problems of Treatment and Care
    A. Nonmedical forms of treatment include traditional psychotherapy, client centered therapy, behavior modification, hypnosis.
    B. Medical treatments of mental illness include the use of chemotherapy and electroconvulsive therapy.
    C. Institutions for treating the mentally ill developed around the beginning of the 20th century.
    D. Community Psychology developed in the 1950s when drugs increased the ability of patients to function outside of hospitals. The development of community resources to aid the patient's life outside of institutions was promoted.
      1. Halfway houses: structured environments in the community were developed.
      2. The civil rights of patients also became important during the community psychology movement.
    E. Deinstitutionalization reversed a trend of increased hospitalization of the mentally ill prevalent in the first half of the 20th century.
      1. The incidence of mental illness has increased although the number of hospitalized patients has decreased.
      2. The problem of the homeless is largely separate from mental illness; only about 10 % of the homeless demonstrate psychiatric disorders. Mental illness may be a response, rather than a cause, of homelessness.
VII. Social Policy
    A. Concerns issues of the treatment of the mentally ill, especially with regards to their rights and the rights of society, as well.
    B. The community treatment centers often failed to provide adequate treatment and resources for patients.
      1. The system was plagued by lack of treatment coordination, ineffective patient monitoring, lack of adequate services and monies.

Key Terms:
Mental Illness: usually refers to mental disorders severe enough to require hospitalization.
Psychosis: severe degree of mental illness in which individuals typically require treatment over a long period of time.
Deinstitutionalization: the discharge of patients from hospitals into the community, often with a failure to

provide adequate community support services.
Medical model: refers to mental disorders being viewed analogously to physical disease.
Neurosis: refers to people who can function in daily life but depend a good deal on psychological defense mechanisms. It is not used, in the DMSIII, as a diagnostic category.
Psychotropic drugs: medications effective in reducing the symptoms of severe mental illness.
Psychotherapy: treatment for mental illness based on promoting insight into deeper psychological motivations.
Total Institutions: control all aspects of daily life such as eating, sleeping, bathing, working, leisure.
Chemotherapy: a variety of drugs used in the treatment of mental illness.

Practice Test:
Multiple Choice Questions: Select the best answer for each question below:
1. Until the mid-twentieth century, many individuals in treatment for mental disorders:
    a. did not need any help
    b. actually had epilepsy or brain tumors
    c. could be expected to get better quickly
    d. suffered little stigma from their patient status.
2. An example of a "mass psychosis" would be:
    a. schizophrenics
    b. epileptics
    c. The People's Temple
    d. none of the above.
3. Which of the following is symptomatic of severe mental illness?
    a. hallucinations
    b. severe mood swings
    c. overwhelming periods of sadness
    d. all of the above.
4. The social construction of mental illness refers to:
    a. definitions derived from social norms
    b. the building of large mental hospitals in the 1950s
    c. the idea that mental illness has concrete criteria for labeling
    d. mental illness is unrelated to social conditions.
5. The medical model of mental illness:
    a. does not require treatment for mental illnesses
    b. is the most established viewpoint
    c. believes mental illnesses require surgical treatment
    d. is utilized only by medical doctors.
6. For which of the following disorders is there evidence of a biological base?
    a. schizophrenia

b. alcoholism
c. manic depression
d. all of the above.
7. A disease concept of mental illness:
a. incorporates the social environment in treatment
b. leads to simple criteria for recovery
c. denies the impact of the social environment
d. is not used in the area of mental disorders today.
8. A view of mental illness as residual deviance was developed by:
a. Thomas Scheff
b. Thomas Szasz
c. Sigmund Freud
d. Carl Jung.
9. The concept of the "myth of mental illness" refers to:
a. the nonexistence of behaviors labeled as mental illness
b. the belief that mental illness labels are largely biased by psychiatrists' values
c. people with symptoms do not require help
d. none of the above.
10. The DSMIII-R is drawn largely from the _____ model of mental illness.
a. medical
b. deviant
c. myth
d. none of the above.
11. D. Rosenhan's study utilizing fake "patients" indicated:
a. that labels have no consequence in the attribution of mental illness
b. doctors' infallible ability to separate the truly ill from the fakes
c. the patients did not identify the fakes
d. the label of a disease can itself effect the view of an individual as mentally ill.
12. Homosexuality:
a. has always been treated as a mental illness
b. does not appear as an illness in the DSMIII
c. is objectively "sick" behavior
d. was not a controversial topic for the APA.
13. People with mental disturbances:
a. are accurately estimated
b. often go untreated in the population
c. are evenly distributed in the population
d. are not overrepresented in poverty populations.
14. The drift theory of mental illness suggests:
a. the mentally ill drift downward in society
b. social class level causes mental illness
c. psychological disturbance is unrelated to mobility
d. none of the above.

15. Electroconvulsive therapy:
    a. is used in cases of severe depression
    b. causes some brain damage
    c. often results in long-term memory loss
    d. all of the above.
16. Chemotherapy:
    a. is largely ineffective in reducing psychotic symptoms
    b. have few physical side effects
    c. has contributed to deinstitutionalization
    d. is an effective treatment by itself.
17. Difficulties in public mental hospitals include:
    a. low salaries
    b. high worker turnover
    c. little doctor/patient contact
    d. all of the above.
18. Which of the following is **not** characteristic of total institutions?
    a. control of all aspects of daily life
    b. loss of self-esteem
    c. loss of self-image developed outside
    d. the probability of benefits from the experience of hospitalization.
19. Deinstitutionalization was facilitated by:
    a. psychotropic drugs
    b. cuts in federal health and welfare programs
    c. little concern for patients' rights
    d. all of the above.
20. In the 1960s:
    a. the number of hospitalized patients increased
    b. the number of hospitalized patients decreased
    c. less people exhibited mental illness
    d. none of the above.
21. The majority of the homeless are mentally ill.
    a. true
    b. false

Essay Questions:
1. Do you think that insanity should be used as a defense in criminal trials?
2. Explain the concept of the "social construction" of mental illness.
3. What is the relationship between poverty and social class?
4. What kind of social policy do you think is needed to adequately address issues of the treatment of the mentally ill?

Test Answers:
Multiple Choice Questions:
1. b
2. c
3. d
4. a
5. b
6. d
7. c
8. a
9. b
10. a
11. d
12. b
13. b
14. a
15. d
16. c
17. d
18. d
19. a
20. b
21. b

Essay Questions: Student should address the following issues:
1. What is the nature of mental illness that could be justified as removing guilt?
 - What is the justice system's responsibility in protecting society?
 - What is the responsibility in the justice system for protecting victims' rights? The rights of the mentally ill?
2. Include discussion of the influence of:
 - social norms determining concepts of normality and illness.
 - consequences of the labeling of people as mentally ill.
 - the influence of poverty and inequality.
 - treating the mentally ill as deviants.
3. Issues addressed should include:
 - stresses of urban life, especially in impoverished areas.
 - the drift hypothesis.
 - social selection theory.
4. Issues discussed should include:
 - national/federal policy development and funds.
 - local resources and funds.
 - the development of an integrated system of treatment which addresses all aspects of patient needs.

CHAPTER FOUR: SEX-RELATED SOCIAL PROBLEMS

Chapter Summary:
 Changing attitudes towards sexual behaviors have made some practices related to sexual activity controversial. The chapter begins with an explanation of how disparate societal views cause social problems in the area of sexuality. One area which traditionally has been viewed as problematic is that of homosexuality. Aspects of homosexuality are examined.
 The chapter also delineates the areas of prostitution and pornography as particularly problematic. Behaviors and problems associated with these areas are also reviewed.
 Finally, social policy with respect to homosexuality, prostitution, and pornography are also examined. The legalization, and modification in the laws in these areas, is looked at in the light of recent research in these areas.

Learning Objectives:
 After studying the chapter the student should be able:
   - to explain why sexual behaviors can be considered to be social problems; attention should be paid to changing values and to the range of behaviors observed.
   - to understand the phenomenon of homosexuality including: its origins; its prevalence; gay identities and subcultures; lesbianism; and societal views.
   - to understand the types of prostitution, societal views of prostitution, sociological views of prostitution, and the self-identity of prostitutes.
   - to explain the nature and functions of pornography, its controversial aspects, and societal views on it.
   - to discuss social policy debate with regard to homosexuality, pornography, and prostitution.

Chapter Outline:
I. Sex as a Social Problem
    A. Attitudes towards sex have changed over the past fifty years but traditional behaviors and views still are present. People particularly have difficulty dealing with the areas of homosexuality, prostitution, and pornography.
    B. Classifications of sex-related social problems are in three categories:
        1. Tolerated Sex Variance: premarital intercourse; heterosexual oral-genital contact; masturbation.
        2. Asocial Sex Variance: incest; child sex molestation; rape; exhibitionism; voyeurism.
        3. Structured Sex Variance: structured behavior with subcultural elements such as homosexuality; pornography; polygyny; prostitution.

II. Homosexuality
A. Defined as a sexual preference for members of one's own sex. General estimates suggest that about 10% of Americans are exclusively, or primarily, homosexual. Homosexuals are often discriminated against in many areas of life. Almost half of Americans polled feel homosexuals should be barred from holding some jobs, particularly those involving contact with young people.
B. The historical view of social scientists has been to view homosexuality as an illness. But Kinsey and others have established that homosexuals cannot be distinguished from heterosexuals in psychological terms. The deviance associated with homosexuality appears to stem from the experience of rejection by the larger society.
C. There is no strong support for the assertion that homosexuality is biologically determined. Human sexual behavior is learned behavior and, as a consequence, social scientists emphasize the social environment. Interactionist theorists emphasize the importance of the label in an individual's self-identification as a homosexual. Homosexuals do not share a particular group of personality characteristics. Homosexuals differ in their willingness to make their sexuality publicly known.
D. It is through contact with admitted homosexuals that most homosexual men gain a gay identity. Gay subculture provides individuals with a way of understanding and accepting their sexual orientation. The gay movement increased momentum in the 1970's but dropped off in the 1980's after the publicity surrounding AIDS.
E. Homosexual women, or lesbians, are much less studied, and noticeable, than are gay men. Lesbianism generally starts later in life than male homosexuality and often is initiated within an emotional relationship.

III. Prostitution
A. Prostitution, or sex on a promiscuous and mercenary basis, is illegal most places in the U.S. Debates are frequent concerning the legalization of prostitution. Proponents argue it is a common occurrence and may as well be supervised. Additionally, it can provide to the reduction of crime.
B. Recent research suggests that many prostitutes were sexually abused before they became prostitutes.
C. Some theorists believe that prostitution is functional deviance in that it allows men to have sexually gratifying experiences without emotional or legal commitments.
D. Many people have posed the question of why some women become prostitutes. Much recent research indicates common histories, among prostitutes, of sexual

abuse. Others have advanced theories relating to poverty backgrounds and simultaneous exposure to prostitutes. Davis shows that many prostitutes were already considered marginal prior to their becoming prostitutes.
   1. Davis' study shows three stages of development of an identity of prostitution:
     a. drift from promiscuity to an initial act of prostitution.
     b. a transitional phase of occasional prostitution and learning some of the skills.
     c. a professional identification usually stemming from a social label of prostitute.
   2. Call-girls usually undergo a period of training by another girl who helps the novice develop a clientele.
E. In the prostitutes' subculture clients are generally seen only in economic terms. A woman's pimp, generally characteristic of streetwalkers, functions as her protector, friend, and "man." Pimps usually completely control their women.

IV. Pornography
A. There is much disagreement on what actually constitutes pornography. Most people agree that the sexual exploitation of children is inexcusable. Many women believe that pornography promotes violence towards women.
B. Social scientists believe that pornography is a problem because it offends sexual norms and has negative effects on the communities in which it is sold.
C. Pornography calls into question issues relating to first amendment rights. Some believe that banning pornography would lead to censorship in other areas. Current laws mandate obscenity in terms of the values of a "reasonable person."
D. Research on pornography has concluded that exposure to pornography does not lead directly to social or individual harm.
E. Some people fear that pornography may lead to rape and other sex-related crimes. So far there is no evidence for this assertion.

V. Social Policy
A. Functionalists view sex-related social problems as a breakdown in norms and institutions controlling sexual behaviors. Interactionist theorists maintain that groups promoting their viewpoints are struggling to get their views to be dominant. Conflict theorists view dissension as inevitable due to groups' different societal positions.
B. Laws fail to protect the rights of homosexuals. A 1976 Supreme Court ruling upheld the rights of states to

prosecute people for private homosexual activity. **The AIDS epidemic has heightened anti-homosexual sentiment.**
C. Some people propose the legalization of prostitution as a means of: reducing the spread of disease; reducing crime-related to prostitution; reduce government corruption; help keep neighborhoods safe. Also, some feel that prostitution is a victimless crime and not punished among upper classes.
D. Some people feel that even if pornography is not directly related to crime, it nevertheless degrades people and harms society.

Key Terms:
Tolerated Sex Variance: acts generally disapproved of but common enough that little sanctioning occurs for those who engage in them.
Asocial Sex Variance: acts that elicit widespread, strong disapproval and which are usually illegal.
Structured Sex Variance: behavior, supported and engaged in by a large number of people, which run counter to prevailing norms and legal statutes.
Lesbians: homosexual women.
Gay Ghetto: neighborhoods, streets, and/or buildings which are predominantly inhabited by homosexuals.
Call Girls: educated, well-dressed, attractive prostitutes who never solicit. They make all arrangements via the telephone.
House Girls: prostitutes who are employed by a madam and work in a house.
Female Hustlers: prostitutes who directly solicit and who value status symbols and good clothes.
Streetwalkers: the lowest type of prostitutes who solicit customers and make the least amount of money.
Pornography: depiction of sexual behavior with the goal of sexually exciting the viewer.

Practice Test
Multiple Choice Questions: Select the best answer for each of the questions below:
1. Which of the following is **NOT** generally seen to be a major sex-related problem today?
    a. pornography
    b. masturbation *(marked)*
    c. prostitution
    d. homosexuality.
2. Incest generally occurs:
    a. only between step-parents and step-children
    b. mostly in the lower socioeconomic classes
    c. only in very rare cases
    d. more commonly in higher socioeconomic levels. *(marked)*

3. Child molestation is:
   a. primarily a homosexual act
   b. usually an act between strangers
   c. usually perpetrated by elderly people
   d. none of the above.
4. Rape is a crime:
   a. of sexual release
   b. of aggression
   c. of only heterosexuals
   d. never found in marriage.
5. Homosexuality appears to be:
   a. a consequence of learning
   b. established at birth
   c. a biological given
   d. characteristic of a particular type of man.
6. Among homosexual men:
   a. very few establish long-term relations
   b. in partner relations, one always plays the "masculine" role
   c. any man engaging in a homosexual act is considered to be a homosexual
   d. none of the above.
7. Recent research indicates that prostitutes:
   a. have a father complex
   b. were victims of parental neglect
   c. were themselves sexually abused
   d. none of the above.
8. Which is the lowest type of prostitution:
   a. call girl
   b. streetwalker
   c. house girl
   d. female hustlers.
9. Current beliefs concerning prostitution include all of the following EXCEPT:
   a. many prostitutes felt alone and friendless
   b. many prostitutes were victimized by rape and/or incest
   c. many prostitutes had no prior sexual experience
   d. runaways frequently turn to prostitution.
10. Which of the following is NOT a concern related to pornography:
    a. it demeans women
    b. it is assumed to be healthy for males
    c. it exploits children
    d. it threatens first amendment rights.
11. Pornography is:
    a. completely illegal
    b. left to the discretion of municipalities
    c. not protected at all by the first amendment
    d. none of the above.

12. Which of the following has been advanced as a use of pornography:
    a. enhancement of one's sex life
    b. dissemination of information
    c. improvement of marital relations
    d. all of the above. *(d marked)*
13. With regard to homosexuality in the U.S.:
    a. no state guarantees gay rights by law
    b. homosexuals are accepted by the armed services
    c. homosexual acts often are illegal *(c marked)*
    d. homosexuals are not discriminated against in hiring practices.
14. Arguments favoring the legalization of prostitution include all of the following EXCEPT:
    a. it would provide additional tax revenues
    b. it would reduce the number of clients *(b marked)*
    c. it would reduce the spread of disease
    d. it would reduce government corruption.

Essay Questions:
1. Do you believe that homosexuality is a social problem?
2. Do you feel that prostitution should be made legal? Why or why not?
3. Do you think that pornography should be legal and available to all? Explain your response.

Test Answers:
Multiple Choice Questions:
1. b
2. d
3. d
4. b
5. a
6. d
7. c
8. b
9. c
10. b
11. b
12. d
13. c
14. b

Essays Questions:
Answers should include addressing the following areas:
1. Is homosexuality (or sexuality) a purely personal matter?
   - Does homosexuality effect a person's job performance (i.e., should it be a factor in gaining employment)?
   - Should any sexual act that does not hurt anyone, and is practiced between consenting adults, be illegal?
   - Why are gay people perceived as threatening?
2. The issue of differential treatment of clients and prostitutes in the legal system should be addressed.
   - Issues of health, economics, and quality of neighborhoods should be included.
3. Issues of the value of women and the concept of sexuality should be addressed.
   - Issues concerning the first amendment also need to be dealt with.
   - The protection of children both from exploitation in pornography and exposure to it also should be included.

CHAPTER FIVE: ALCOHOL AND OTHER DRUGS

Chapter Summary:

The chapter begins with a consideration of what the term "drug" refers to. The nature of drug use and abuse is then reviewed. The prevalence and patterning of drug use is examined, as well as problems relating to it. The case of alcohol abuse is given special attention. Alcohol use is so common and causes so many problems, especially in terms of health and accidents, that it is a focal point of public concern.

The use and abuse of illegal substances is discussed. Attention is given to marijuana and other kinds of popularly used illegal substances. The abuse of legal substances is also discussed. The incidence and treatment of drug abuse is discussed.

The chapter ends with a discussion of social policy with regard to drug use. The laws pertaining to alcohol use have been increasingly restrictive. Policy debates regarding illegal substances are discussed as there are controversial suggestions for their modification.

Learning Objectives:

After studying the chapter the student should be able:
- to define what is meant by drug addiction and dependence and provide examples of each.
- to explain the nature, problems, and treatment associated with abuse of alcohol; included in this would be a comprehension of the scope of the problem and problems resulting from the abuse.
- to identify the types of illegal drugs that exist and the properties and effects of their use and abuse.
- to understand patterns of drug use, social problems associated with it, and modes of treatment.
- to explain drug policy, particularly in terms of law enforcement, and to elaborate criticisms of current policy.

Chapter Outline:
I. The Nature of the Problem
 A. In a pharmacological sense, a drug is any substance that alters the structure of a living organism. More specifically, a drug is any habit-forming substance that affects physiological functions, mood, perceptions, or consciousness. Additionally, it has the potential for misuse and/or of causing harm to the user.
 B. Drug abuse refers to the use of unacceptable and/or illegal substances. It also refers to excessive or inappropriate use of legal substances. Drug use has an objective and subjective dimension. Many people per-

ceive marijuana, for example, as dangerous even though objectively alcohol and nicotine are more so.
C. Drug addiction specifically refers to the physical need to continue using a substance. Many people develop a drug dependence, or a psychological/habitual need for a substance but are not physically addicted.

II. Alcohol Use and Abuse
A. Alcohol is a drug that has become integrated into many people's lifestyle. Alcohol is a dangerous drug. There are many Americans who are problem drinkers. There are also many alcohol addicted, or alcoholic, Americans. There is some evidence of a genetic link in alcoholism.
B. Demographic studies of alcohol consumption suggest that young men in higher socioeconomic statuses drink more than other age groups. Men drink more than women, on the whole. Yet, the number of women having problems with alcohol is growing. As a group, Catholics demonstrate a tendency for more alcohol consumption than other religious denominations. There are ethnic variations in drinking patterns that have been documented. Familial patterns of drinking behavior have also been documented.
C. Drinking among youth has become a focal point of concern in the last two decades. Six percent of American teens drink daily, according to one study.
D. Problems associated with alcohol abuse include:
   1. health problems: alcohol has a high caloric content but little nutritional value; it lowers resistance to infectious disease; causes liver damage; causes heart ailments and is related to cancer; is implicated in some suicides.
   2. alcohol is a factor in one-half of fatal vehicular accidents and serious injury accidents.
   3. a relationship to about 16% of arrests for nonserious crimes; a high rate of relationship to homicides.
   4. a negative effect on the family in terms of emotional development and, often, in terms of poverty resulting from job loss.
   5. about 5% of alcoholics end up on skid row.
E. Treatment of alcohol problems generally includes both medical intervention for the alcohol withdrawal and the modification of underlying problems which caused the drug abuse.
   1. Alcoholics Anonymous is a self-help group of recovering alcoholics. Founded in 1935, it has been helpful to many in keeping them sober.
   2. Antabuse is a controversial drug used in some treatment. It causes strong physical reactions if mixed

with alcohol. It is used in aversion methods of treatment.

    3. Employee Assistance Programs are proving effective in treating alcohol problems in the workplace.

III. Illegal Drug Use and Abuse

  A. Marijuana is the most widely used illegal substance. There is little evidence that it leads to the use of stronger drugs.

  B. Cocaine, and crack, widely associated with use in upper socioeconomic classes are being used more now in working and middle classes. Taken in large quantities over time, they can cause paranoid psychoses.

  C. Heroin is addictive and highly related to crime because of the vast expense associated with maintaining a habit.

  D. Hallucinogens, popularly associated with LSD. No adequate data exists on the physical or psychological consequences of these drugs.

  E. Amphetamines are stimulants, which are legal when prescribed by physicians. Many people become addicted through prescriptive use of these drugs; withdrawal can cause suicidal depression.

  F. Barbiturates are depressants and can cause poisoning, especially if mixed with alcohol. People frequently alternate the use of amphetamines and barbiturates.

IV. Patterns and Problems of Drug Abuse

  A. Patterns of drug use have changed in the past 10-15 years. Exposure to drug users is the first step in trying drugs. Marijuana use, by youths, has decreased significantly in the past 10 years. The proportion of youth (12-17 years) using cocaine has increased in the 1980s while use in the 18-25 year category has decreased. Drug use is still widespread, with 37% of Americans using an illegal substance in the past year. Overall, however, drug use in the 1980s has decreased.

  B. The most important influence in drug use is the influence of peer groups. Other conditions, such as family, school, and environment, are also important. Marijuana is not, as previously suspected, a stepping stone to other drugs.

  C. Marijuana, and low use of bartiturates are not associated with crime or violence. Amphetamine users are disproportionately involved in violent crimes. Heroin users are the most frequently associated group of drug users involved in crime. Most of these crimes are money-seeking or drug-trafficking crimes.

  D. Intravenous drug use is highly associated with the spread of AIDS among heterosexuals.

    E. Drug use can be helped by treatment. The changing of an individual's social milieu is particularly helpful in changing drug use.
    F. Therapeutic communities, which help the reentry into social life, have been helpful in drug treatment. Many of these are staffed by ex-addicts and provide counseling for psychological difficulties and provide educational and vocational programs.
    G. Methadone maintenance is a controversial treatment for heroin addiction. Methadone is itself addicting but does not produce a "high."
V. Social Policy
    A. Chemical abuse social policies consist of:
      1. Control policies focusing on helping the individual control their behaviors and/or providing local services.
      2. Law enforcement efforts to deal with the problem more effectively.
    B. Arrests of alcoholics appear to promote drug use through labeling the individual as an alcoholic and creating secondary deviance.
    C. The public has exerted pressure for greater punishment of drunk drivers. Educational efforts, increased age of legal drinking, sobriety checks, and greater legal sanctions for drunk driving have decreased alcohol-related auto fatalities.
    D. Greater law enforcement techniques have not been useful in the reduction of illegal drug use. "Get-tough" laws have caused youths to become more important in drug trafficking because of mandatory sentences for adults.
    E. Many feel that drug laws should be revised to be more realistic. This has been argued especially in favor of the decriminalization of marijuana. Some people advocate the change in laws concerning hard drugs, as a means to curtail drug-related crimes and to protect citizens' rights.

Key Terms:
Drug: any habit-forming substance that affects physiological functions, mood, perception, or consciousness; has potential for misuse; may be harmful to the user.
Drug Abuse: the use of unacceptable drugs and/or the excessive or inappropriate use of acceptable drugs.
Addiction: physical dependence on a drug; discontinuation would result in withdrawal symptoms.
Drug Dependence: psychological dependence, habitual use of a substance; lack of use results in discomfort but not in physical withdrawal.
Crack: a form of cocaine that can be smoked.

Hallucinogens: drugs that distort the user's perceptions; often associated with visual hallucinogens.
Amphetamines: drugs referred to as uppers, act as stimulants.
Barbiturates: drugs which depress the Central Nervous System.

Practice Test:
Multiple Choice Questions: Select the best answer for each question below:
1. Which of the following substances is **NOT** usually considered to be a drug:
    a. caffeine
    b. nicotine
    c. sugar
    d. alcohol.
2. Which of the following may be considered drug abuse:
    a. consistent use of prescriptive tranquillizers
    b. use of cocaine several times a week
    c. daily alcohol consumption
    d. all of the above.
3. Drug dependence refers to:
    a. psychological need for a substance
    b. physical addiction
    c. both psychological and physical needs
    d. none of the above.
4. Which of the following statements is **NOT** true:
    a. alcohol is the most used drug in America
    b. withdrawal from alcohol is not dangerous
    c. there is evidence of a genetic link in alcoholism
    d. problem drinkers are not physically addicted to alcohol.
5. Which group is **UNLIKELY** to have high rates of alcohol consumption:
    a. young businessmen
    b. married working women
    c. farmers
    d. Catholics.
6. Which of the following is **NOT** a problem associated with alcohol abuse:
    a. ill health
    b. family disorganization
    c. emotional problems in adult children of alcoholic parent(s)
    d. none of the above.
7. Alcoholics Anonymous:
    a. is an organization begun 10 years ago
    b. is ineffective in keeping people sober
    c. builds self-esteem and operates on a quasireligious model

d.   none of the above.
8. Which program has been effective in treating **drinking** problems in the workplace:
   a. Employee Assistance Programs
   b. Alcoholics Anonymous
   c. Rehabilitation Programs
   d. Antabuse Programs.
9. Which of the following drug use is associated with the greatest physical danger:
   a. heroin
   b. barbiturates
   c. marijuana
   d. LSD.
10. Marijuana use among youth:
    a. peaked in the mid-1980s
    b. peaked in the late 1970s
    c. is currently on the increase
    d. is as popular as ever.
11. Overall drug use in the 1980s has:
    a. increased since the 1960s and 1970s
    b. decreased since the 1960s and 1970s
    c. remained equivalent to the 1960s and 1970s
    d. none of the above.
12. The drug most often associated with **VIOLENT** crime is:
    a. marijuana
    b. amphetamines
    c. barbiturates
    d. heroin.
13. Which of the following statements concerning drug treatment is correct:
    a. "once an addict always an addict"
    b. there are no successful treatment programs
    c. changing an addict's social milieu is essential
    d. none of the above.
14. Methadone programs are:
    a. widely acclaimed for their usefulness
    b. accused of attempting to be a form of social control of addicts
    c. good because they end addiction to substances
    d. drug free.
15. Social policy efforts focus mostly on:
    a. law enforcement to reduce problems
    b. the legalization of more drugs
    c. making alcohol illegal
    d. none of the above.
16. Which of the following alcohol-related strategies has been used to decrease motor vehicle fatalities:
    a. increased age of legal drinking
    b. educational programs for first offenders
    c. sobriety checks on the roads

    d. all of the above.

Essay Questions:
1. Do you think that drug dependency is a big problem in the U.S.? Explain your response.
2. Do you think that alcohol and drug abuse treatment should be supported by public funding? Explain your response.
3. Do you think illegal substances should be made legal or decriminalized? Explain your response.

Test Answers:
Multiple Choice Questions:
1. c
2. d
3. a
4. b
5. c
6. d
7. c
8. a
9. b
10. b
11. b
12. b
13. c
14. b
15. a
16. d

Essay Answers: Student should address the following issues:
1. Address the incidence of drug abuse, including use of alcohol, nicotine, and caffeine.
 - Discuss psychological issues underlying drug use and those resulting from its use.
 - Discuss the relation of American lifestyles to drug use.
2. Issues of the cost, financially and otherwise, of drug use should be considered.
 - Discussion of responsibility for addiction should also be discussed.
3. Marijuana use should be addressed, particularly in relation to its safety as compared with alcohol.
 - Drugs, and their relation to crime, should also be considered.
 - The British system of treating narcotic addiction should also be included in the discussion.
 - Issues of morality and individual rights should be considered.

CHAPTER SIX: CRIME AND CRIMINALS

Chapter Summary:
The chapter begins with a discussion of the ways in which crime rates are counted in the U.S. Official crime rates focus on some crimes and omit others. The categorization of different types of crimes is reviewed in terms of the type of crimes committed and the type of offender.

The consideration of the causes of crime is the next theories are briefly reviewed and current demographic trends and sociological explanations are discussed. The American system has focused on punishment and deterring crime and only recently has focused on rehabilitation. The efforts of controlling crime and the nature of the criminal justice system are explored.

The chapter ends with a discussion of how social policy could address the needs of an overcrowded, and often detrimental, prison system.

Learning Objectives:
After studying the chapter the student should be able:
- to explain what constitutes crime and what factors go into establishing official crime rates.
- to identify types/categories of crime and explain what type of individuals participate in each, and how the society views each.
- to elaborate demographic information on crime and to explain sociological views of criminality.
- to understand the history of controlling crime in the U.S. as one primarily concerned with retribution and deterrence; to identify efforts in the rehabilitation of criminals.
- to explain social policy issues, particularly their differential implementation with regard to street criminals versus white collar criminals.

Chapter Outline:
I. The Nature of Crime
   A. The Crime Index and the Uniform Crime Reports (UCR) are official documents concerning the increase of crime. They do not report on the extent of organized and occupational crimes. Crime, in the U.S., is grossly underreported.
   B. Criminal law refers to acts prohibited and punishable with particular sanctions. Civil law refers to noncriminal acts in which one individual injures another.
   C. Although crimes are codified by laws, in practice criminality is determined by the beliefs of the police. Police possess considerable discretion in regard to what

laws to enforce and to what extent they will be enforced.
  1. In a well-known study of delinquent youths, W. Chambliss found that local police and community bias had a pervasive effect on the interpretations of youths' acts according to social class lines. Rates of misbehavior between youth groups studied were similar. The rate of detection, punishment, and labeling was much higher for the working class group than for the middle class group.
 D. UCR statistics indicate a higher criminal rate for minorities than for whites. However, it should be kept in mind that the reports deal only with people apprehended for crimes. Self-report studies indicate equivalent crime rates across racial lines. A review of 35 studies indicated that social class cannot be used to predict the likelihood of involvement in criminal activity. Some theorists speculate that the upper classes actually have a higher crime rate than the lower socioeconomic statuses.
II. Types of Crimes and Criminals
 A. Violent personal crimes are those in which physical injury is inflicted or threatened. Crime rates in this area are very high. While many robberies occur between strangers, murders often occur between friends and relatives. Two-thirds of the total violent crimes occur between strangers.
 B. Occasional property crimes are committed by unsophisticated persons usually working alone. Such crimes include vandalism, shoplifting, and check forgery.
 C. Occupation, or white collar, crime is lawbreaking in the usual course of business activity. It is largely ignored by society but probably common. It includes such things as embezzlement, fraud, false advertising, price-fixing, insiders' trading, and antitrust violations. It is generally learned through association with others already practicing it.
 D. Conventional crimes are those that are semi-professional in technique and often committed by young adults. They include robbery, larceny, burglary, and gang theft. The people committing these crimes move into criminal life gradually. As they develop criminal records, they are progressively defined as criminals. Once they gain this identification, it is difficult to reenter the mainstream of society.
 E. Organized crime is a rational system of illegal activities devised by a large organization to maximize profits. Organized crime provides goods and services to the public that cannot be legally obtained. Major

sources of profit come from illegal gambling, loan sharking, and narcotics trade. Some organized crime members also engage in legitimate enterprises primarily to establish a tax cover. Much of the success of organized crime is dependent on the cooperation of corrupt officials.
F. Professional crime is committed by sophisticated, clever criminals who are seldom caught. Many of these people come from higher social strata and make a living from illegal activities.
G. Juvenile law is designed to protect and redirect youthful offenders. This is based on the assumption that youth are devoid of "criminal intent." This assumption is often criticized today as is the latitude of the juvenile court system.

III. Conditions and Causes of Crime
  A. Up through the late nineteenth century, criminality was ascribed to the physical characteristics of the criminal. Today, some people believe that certain inherited characteristics predispose individuals to criminal activity. This idea, often related in terms of an extra Y chromosome, remain controversial.
  B. Men have been far more likely to commit crimes than women. The rate of increase in female criminality has been higher, in recent years, than male increases. Causes have been attributed to greater social equality, greater economic pressure, and greater drug use.
  C. Youth is more highly correlated with crime than any other factor. Some people seem to give up crime in their late 20s and early 30s. This has been attributed to maturation and family responsibility.
  D. Because demographic characteristics do not adequately account for crime rates, sociologists have developed their own theoretical views of crime.
    1. Conflict theorists look at inequalities and perceptions of deprivation and view crime in terms of rebellion against the system. Criminality appears to be concentrated in lower socioeconomic statuses but such assertions are not defensible given the current state of crime reporting. Blacks are overrepresented in rates of arrest, convictions, imprisonment for street crimes. They are also more likely to report being victims of crime. Higher arrest rates remain even when socioeconomic status is considered.
    2. Functionalists view criminality in terms of goals-and-opportunities approach. Theorists, most notably R. Merton, believe that people who aspire to the material aspirations of the society will try to attain these through illegal means if they see their legitimate channels as blocked. This anomie theory focuses on the

disparity between goals and means.
3. Interactionist theories look at the processes by which people internalize norms. Differential association looks at the learning process of the individual. If people close to the individual favor criminal behavior, the individual will also lean to do so. Delinquent subcultures help to redefine values not applicable to people at lower ends of the status ladder.

IV. Controlling Crime

A. The American prison system is still largely punitive. Rehabilitation only recently became a concern of the criminal justice system. The system is geared towards retribution and deterrence. Punishment is viewed as "paying" for one's crime and also as a deterrent to others. If the punishment is severe, and people feel certain they will get caught, punishment can decrease the likelihood of committing a crime.

B. There is no evidence that rehabilitative efforts are more successful at reducing recidivism than punitive measures. The prison system itself may be a hindrance to rehabilitation. Work-release programs appear effective in helping inmates and in reducing the cost of custodial facilities.

C. Crime prevention includes efforts to improve a person's social environment; efforts to reduce the youth's exposure to illegal and antisocial acts; the prevention of further delinquency through program development. There appears to be some positive outcome of counseling youth but not of the desired magnitude. Some people feel the family and community should receive better support to help the youth rather than incarcerating the youths.

D. Incapacitation has been advanced as a method of prohibiting high-rate offenders from committing more crimes. Difficulties stem from identifying high-risk offenders and from the lack of prison capacity to meet the needs of long-term incarceration.

V. Social Policy

A. Most cases are resolved through plea bargaining. This releases the courts from expensive and long trials. Plea bargaining has been criticized for giving mild sentences for serious offenses.

B. Proposals to reduce occupational crime rates include increasing the penalties; increasing the likelihood of doing time; changing the laws to make them more difficult to break; and stronger enforcement.

C. Organized crime involves one-fourth of the FBI work forces and is hindered by the difficulties with obtaining evidence for court trials.

D. Critics of the criminal justice system have

suggested reducing the status offenses of juveniles and public-order offenses.
E. Recent trends have returned to a focus on confinement and to stricter law enforcement. Overcrowding in the prisons causes violence and mitigates against long prison sentences.

Key Terms:
Uniform Crime Report (UCR): official crime rate document of the FBI, including only crimes reported to the police.
Crime Index: data on the most serious and frequently committed crimes including murder and nonnegligent manslaughter, forcible rape, robbery, aggravated assault, burglary, larceny-theft, motor vehicle theft, and arson.
Crime: act or omission of an act for which the state can apply sanctions.
Criminal Law: prohibits certain acts and prescribes punishments for violators.
Civil Law: noncriminal acts in which one person injures another.
Violent Personal Crime: acts in which physical injury is inflicted or threatened.
Embezzlement: theft from one's employer.
Fraud: obtaining money under false pretenses.
Occupational Crime: illegal acts committed in the process of normal business activities.
Public Order Crimes: those acts which violate the customs of the community.
Organized Crime: a rational system of illegal activities enacted by a large organization.
Differential Association: learning to become delinquent because of the excess of definitions of behavior favorable to law breaking among significant others.
Recidivism: rates of recurrences of crime.
Plea Bargaining: wherein the offender agrees to plead guilty to a lesser crime and thereby relieves the courts from conducting a trial.
Status Offenses: juvenile behaviors that would not be crimes in adulthood.

Practice Test:
Multiple Choice Questions:
Select the best answer for each question below.
1. Which type of crime does **NOT** appear in the Crime Index:
    a. violent crime
    b. occupational crimes
    c. sex offenses
    d. property crimes.
2. A study of delinquent youths by Chambliss indicated:
    a. poor kids are clearly the good guys

b. poor kids are clearly the bad guys
   c. there was little actual differences in delinquent activity between socioeconomic statuses
   d. none of the above.
3. Which of the following conclusively has been shown to influence crime rates:
   a. police perceptions
   b. racial factors
   c. socioeconomic status
   d. none of the above.
4. Which crime category is said to have the largest number of criminal (at least according to current data):
   a. public order crimes
   b. violent crimes
   c. occupational crimes
   d. conventional crimes.
5. Which group of offenders is MOST likely to gain a self-concept, and societal view, of a criminal:
   a. occupational criminals
   b. organized criminals
   c. public order criminals
   d. conventional criminals.
6. Which of the following statements about organized crime is TRUE:
   a. it operates largely on the basis of supply and demand
   b. it is based on profits from gambling, loan sharking, and drug trade
   c. it is dependent on the cooperation of corrupt officials
   d. all of the above.
7. Biological theories of criminality:
   a. are no longer adhered to by anyone
   b. were prevalent in, medieval times
   c. are not found in the 19th century
   d. none of the above.
8. Which of the following is TRUE:
   a. more old people commit crimes
   b. women's criminality is increasing
   c. women now comprise 23% of prison populations
   d. crime rates increase for people in their late 20s.
9. Assertions that lower classes are responsible for more crime than others:
   a. are agreed upon by all
   b. are influenced by police bias
   c. show no relation between crime and poverty
   d. show the same differences in serious and nuisance offenses.
10. Anomie theory of criminality:
    a. is a functionalist theory

43

    b. ignores people's sociodemographic characteristics
    c. ignores discrimination in society
    d. is not interested in the crimes of the poor.
11. Which of the following is believed by some to be elements of lower-class culture which produce delinquency:
    a. community status
    b. emphasis on masculinity
    c. belief in fate
    d. all of the above.
12. Punishment for crime serves all of the following functions **EXCEPT**:
    a. paying for one's crime
    b. to deter others from crime
    c. to reinforce the value of conformity
    d. none of the above.
13. Work-release programs:
    a. increases prison costs
    b. are inconsistent with attempts at rehabilitation
    c. are found in almost all states today
    d. none of the above.
14. Cases brought against a person for a crime:
    a. usually end with charges being dropped
    b. usually end in a trial
    c. normally end with plea bargaining
    d. account for one-half of all reported crimes.
15. Juvenile status offenders:
    a. become habitual offenders
    b. do not necessarily commit serious adult crimes
    c. constitute a very small proportion of juvenile offenses
    d. none of the above.

Essay Questions:
1. Discuss the difficulties involved with arriving at accurate crime rates.
2. Why do you think people commit crimes?
3. If you had the power to do so, would you reform the criminal justice system? If so, explain how and why. If not, why not.

Test Answers:
Multiple Choice Questions:
1. b
2. c
3. a
4. a
5. d
6. d
7. b
8. b
9. b
10. a
11. d
12. d
13. c
14. c
15. b

Essay Questions: Student answers should address the following issues:
1. The bias in perception of what acts are typically considered to be crimes.
   - Bias in views of minorities, poor, working classes.
   - The greater perception of threat from street crime vs. white collar crimes.
2. Issues of rates of undetected crimes (making crime rates more universal).
   - Issues of reactions to inequality and perceived deprivation.
   - Exposure to socialization influences conducive to the commitment of crimes.
   - Blocked opportunity of some groups to achieve societal goals.
3. Issues concerning bias in who is apprehended and sentenced.
   - Issues of plea bargaining.
   - Issues of the negative impact of incarceration.
   - Issues concerning selective incapacitation.
   - Issues of developing alternative programs.
   - Issues concerning the protection of citizens.
   - Issues of injustice concerning the lack of punishment for white collar criminals.

CHAPTER SEVEN: VIOLENCE

Chapter Summary:

The chapter begins with a consideration of the history of violence in the U.S. Societal views of the nature of violence are discussed. Explanations of violence, particularly biological versus sociological explanations, are then considered. Attention is paid to the effects of the media on violence in society.

The nature and types of criminal violence are reviewed. The difficulties surrounding establishing accurate incidences of violent crimes are explained. Other forms of violence in the society are discussed next. These include the issue of family violence, both spouse and child abuse, and acts of terrorism.

The chapter ends with a discussion of policy proposals to reduce violence. Chief among these is the proposal for greater gun control legislation.

Learning Objectives:

After studying the chapter the student should be able:
- to explain the history and view of violence in U.S.
- to identify major approaches or theories explaining the prevalence of violence in society.
- to identify the characteristics of criminal violence in the U.S.
- to identify forms of family violence and address the prevalence and nature of family violence.
- to understand the history, origins, and nature of terrorist activities.
- to explain various proposals to deal with violence through social policies.

Chapter Outline:
I. Violence in American History
   A. Violence in the U.S. is exceptionally high as evidenced by homicide rates 20 times those found in England, France, or Japan. Rape, assault, and robbery rates also are very high in the U.S.
II. The Concept of Violence
   Violence may be perceived as legitimate or illegitimate depending on who is using it and why and how.
   Different types of violence include:
   A. Structural Violence: one group exploits another.
   B. Institutional Violence: which protects the state.
   C. Noninstitutional Violence: of those opposed to established authority.
III. Explanations of Violence
   A. Some theorists believe that violence is inherent or instinctual. Others feel that aggression, which is

adaptive, may be natural to humans but not violence.
B. Some theorists believe that violence results from frustration. Common causes of frustration are failure, lack of affection, and poverty. Critics feel that this view fails to account for times when frustration does not lead to violence.
   1. Closely related to the frustration theory is control theory. This view holds that violence results from unsatisfactory relations with others.
C. Many sociologists believe violence to be a learned behavior. They believe that some subcultures promote violent attitudes and acts. Tendencies towards aggression seem to be transmitted intergenerationally in the family. This supports the learning theory of violence.
D. Rational-choice theories of violence see an actor's choice of violence as conscious or unconscious weighing of costs and benefits.
E. Television programming depicts much violence and many killings. Each hour of prime time T.V. has an average of five acts of violence. Studies on the effects of T.V. showing indicate links to short-term violence. Links with long term violence are debated.

IV. Criminal Violence
A. People who commit murders generally do not have criminal records. Most murderers are young men of the same race as their victims. Sixteen percent of all murders are between related persons. Serial murders appear to be committed by psychotic persons. Mass murders are becoming more frequent. Assaults can unintentionally end in homicide.
B. Robberies are the only major crime which typically occurs interracially, between classes, and between strangers.
C. Rape is underreported largely due to women's fear, shame, and mistreatment in the courts. Rape conviction rates are low and this often acts as a deterrent as well. Additional services, such as counseling and specially trained police officers, are increasingly available to rape victims.

V. Family Violence
A. Child abuse is common in the U.S., and it is estimated that only 10%-25% of cases are reported. Corporal punishment is common, and often approved of, in the U.S. The family is cloaked in privacy and the rights of parents to govern their children is upheld. Although child abuse is found among all social classes, environmental and familial characteristics associated with poverty typify many cases. One study indicates that parents who abuse their children tend to demand more from them than is appropriate for their ages.

  B. Spouse abuse more commonly is perpetrated against wives. This is supported as "normal" family behavior, aided by privacy issues in family life, and by the reluctance of authorities to intervene. Women sex-role learning sometimes contributes to their passivity in leaving an abusive relationship. The self-esteem of battered women is severely reduced through the violence.
VI. Gangs, Guns, and Violent Death
  A. Reasons for the U.S. high homicide rate include juvenile violence patterns, available firepower, and lack of consensus on control of lethal weapons.
VII. Social Policy
  A. Recently there has been a great demand for stricter supervision of firearms. This includes more federal legislation of the purchase and sale of firearms. The National Rifle Association, a strong lobby in the capitol, opposes regulation. The U.S. leads all Western nations in rate of homicide, suicide, and accidents by gun. The majority of Americans surveyed favor stricter gun control. Opponents say gun possession is not the cause of murder. Yet, where gun control exists, murder rates have decreased.
  B. Other policy proposals are to limit television violence. Although T.V. networks have agreed to limit prime time violence, the overall influence is reduced by video cassette recorders and cable television.
  C. Family violence appears to be somewhat responsive to efforts at counseling. Programs geared to the training of parents, through programs on parenting skills, appear to be effective. This is particularly so if there are follow-up programs. For spouse abuse, the need for shelters and active intervention is impeded by lack of public funding. Greater reporting of abuse, and coordination of agency efforts, is needed to deal with abuse problems in the family.
  D. Means of dealing with terrorism are not agreed upon. Some people stress direct confrontation while others support negotiation.

Key Terms:
Genocide: systematic termination of a group of people.
Violence: behavior designed to inflict injury to people or damage to property.
Structural Violence: the dominance of one group over another with exploitation built into institutions.
Institutional violence: violence on behalf of or in protection of the state.
Noninstitutional violence: violence by those who are against the established authority.
Murder: unlawful killing of a person with malice afore-

thought.
Manslaughter: unlawful homicide without malice aforethought.
Assault: threat or attempt to injure.
Forcible Rape: forcing sexual intercourse on another against their will.
Statutory Rape: sexual intercourse with a woman under an age set by the state.
Robbery: taking another person's property by intimidation.
Child Abuse: physical injury to a child perpetrated by any person acting as a caretaker.

Practice Test:
Multiple Choice Questions:
Select the best answer for each question below.
1. Deadly violence in the U.S. is:
   a. lower than in other industrialized nations.
   b. higher than in other industrialized nations.
   c. only committed by insane persons.
   d. only perpetrated against strangers.
2. Noninstitutional violence occurs:
   a. when the state is viewed as working against general welfare
   b. when the institutions are contradicting each other
   c. commonly in the U.S. in the 1980s
   d. none of the above.
3. Which characteristic best describes murderers:
   a. being inherently violent
   b. having extensive criminal histories
   c. having extensive impulses toward aggression
   d. having an excess, or deficiency, in control.
4. Subcultures promoting violence would probably include:
   a. juvenile gangs
   b. male sex-role learning
   c. some competitive sports
   d. all of the above.
5. Television violence:
   a. has no known behavioral consequences
   b. has no relation to tolerance of violence in others
   c. promotes short-term violence
   d. none of the above.
6. Which statement is TRUE:
   a. Interracial murders are common
   b. mass murder is becoming more frequent
   c. older men are more likely to murder than younger men
   d. you are least likely to be murdered in the South U.S.
7. Which of the following crimes is MOST likely to occur between strangers:

a. robbery
   b. rape
   c. murder
   d. assault.
8. Rape is a crime:
   a. of passion
   b. of violence
   c. relatively easy to convict on
   d. grossly overreported.
9. Child abuse:
   a. is uncommon in the U.S.
   b. rates are difficult to estimate because of privacy
   c. is unrelated to corporal punishment
   d. is only perpetrated by mothers.
10. Wife abuse is:
    a. estimated to occur to 2 million women every year
    b. promoted by images of marriage in the culture
    c. complicated by the loss of the woman's self-esteem
    d. all of the above.
11. Violent acts by cult groups appear to be facilitated by:
    a. the charismatic leadership of a devinely inspired individual
    b. the group's integration into the mainstream of society
    c. political beliefs
    d. none of the above.
12. The U.S. has:
    a. increased gun control in all states.
    b. seen a decrease in juvenile crime and gangs.
    c. increased the number of households possessing handguns.
    d. a majority of homicides with weapons other than guns.
13. Which of the following statements about guns is **NOT** true:
    a. the NRA is a strong lobby against gun control
    b. gun control decreases rates of handgun murders
    c. U.S. leads Western nations in deaths by guns
    d. none of the above.
14. Parenting skills groups for abusive parents:
    a. are ineffective
    b. helpful, particularly while the child is in foster care
    c. are not necessary once a child is returned to the parents
    d. none of the above.

Essay Questions:
1. Give your response to the quote in the text: "No person living today can question the statement that man, Homo sapiens, self-proclaimed to represent the pinnacle of

evolution, is the most dangerous living species" (Boelkins & Heiser, 1970:15).
2. What do you think is the root of family violence and how do you think it can be addressed?
3. Where do you stand on the issue of gun control (pro or con)?

Test Answers:
Multiple Choice:
1. b
2. a
3. d
4. d
5. c
6. b
7. a
8. b
9. b
10. d
11. a
12. c
13. d
14. b

Essay Questions:
Answers should address the following issues:
1. Issues of where violence comes from, is it inherent, learned, or both?
 - What is the difference between aggression and violence?
 - Are other primates aggressive or violent?
 - What is the relationship between "civilization" and violence?
2. Deal with issues of stress in the family, and outside the family.
 - Address the privatization of the family.
 - Address power dynamics in the family (Adult/Child; Male/Female).
 - Discuss alternatives such as counseling, better daycare and community centers.
3. Are guns "cause" or "symptom" of violence?
 - Gun control appears to reduce murder, by gun, rates.
 - Why is the U.S. gun homicide, suicide, accident rate so high?

CHAPTER EIGHT: POVERTY AMID AFFLUENCE

Chapter Summary:
Poverty in the U.S. is persistent in spite of the status of the U.S. as the wealthiest nation in the world. The chapter begins with a discussion of the nature of the poor and the affluent in the U.S. A discussion of the development of welfare, and the nature of work in the U.S., follows. The determination of poverty levels and who is considered to be impoverished is addressed next. This is followed by a discussion of the concomitants of poverty. These include discrimination in the areas of education, health, housing, opportunity, and other related areas of life.
Theoretical perspectives on the perpetuation of poverty follow. These focus on the nature of structural versus cultural explanations. The nature of current welfare programs is discussed. The Reagan administration's stand is also reviewed. Finally, potential modifications in the country's policies and programs are presented.

Learning Objectives:
After studying the chapter the student should be able:
- to explain the affluence of the U.S. compared to other nations and the prevalence of poverty in the U.S.
- to understand the meaning of the concept of the welfare state.
- to explain the nature and extent of social stratification in the U.S. social class system.
- to describe the poor, in the U.S., in terms of sociodemographic characteristics (race, employment, geographic location, sex).
- to describe concomitants of poverty, especially in terms of education, housing, health, and justice.
- to explain cultural versus structural explanations of poverty.
- to identify social policy issues in regard to poverty and to describe the Reagan administration's conservative viewpoints.

Chapter Outline:
I. The Haves and the Have-Nots
   A. The U.S., by any number of measures, is the most affluent nation in the world. Wealth is concentrated among the few and the number of people experiencing poverty has increased. Equality of opportunity is basic to American ideals but equality of outcome is not. Deprivation, in the U.S. includes inequality in education, housing, healthcare, police protection, jobs, legal justice, nutrition, and other areas.

B. The U.S. has developed into a welfare state. The initial programs that facilitated this development were found in FDR's New Deal policies. Later, LBJ's Great Society programs extended the policy of government aid. Still, the wealthy have legitimate means by which they can avoid paying taxes.
C. The U.S. has the means to eliminate poverty. Yet, policies actually aid in the increase of impoverished citizens. Social scientists believe that poverty will get worse in the near future. Factors such as technological change, lack of adequate income redistribution, and American attitudes toward poverty are advanced to support this idea.
  1. Many Americans believe that the poor are to blame for their poverty. They feel the poor are lazy and do not want to work.
  2. Unemployment is higher among minorities by at least double the rate of white unemployment. Median minority income is about 60-70% of the median income of white households.

II. Poverty and Social Class
A. Society is divided into different strata or hierarchical positions, especially in relation to access to goods and services. Different social classes in the U.S. possess varying degrees of education, occupational prestige, and income. There is both an objective and subjective dimension to social class. The proportion of people who classify themselves as poor is significantly lower than those so classified by the U.S. Census Bureau.
B. Social welfare programs promise to reduce inequality in the U.S. but the 1970s and 1980s have reversed that trend.

III. The Nature of Poverty
A. Poverty means many things to social scientists beyond lack of sufficient money. Poverty can cause feelings of degradation, loss of self-esteem, feelings of resignation, and lack of control.
B. The poverty line was set, in 1965, by determining a food budget and multiplying that figure by three. The official 1990 figure, $12,092 for a family of four, established 13.1% of the population as impoverished. If poverty levels were established by counting people living on less than 1/2 of the median income, then 20% of the population is poor.
C. Who comprise the poor? The poor are:
  1. 23% of all pre-school children;
  2. a disproportionate rate of blacks and other minorities;
  3. inner city people and rural people;

4. poor on welfare often stay on welfare for short periods, have legitimate children, often are women heading households, and have less than three children;
       5. the working poor, are the majority of the poor, and work but do not make sufficient incomes.
IV. Concomitants of Poverty
    A. Poor suffer ill health, high infant mortality rates, lack of insurance coverage, poor healthcare. Present policies governing Medicaid actually encourage the poor to stay on welfare.
    B. Poor children receive less education than other children. Pre-school programs have been effective in counteracting the effects of poverty in education.
    C. The poor often live in substandard housing. Vermin, inadequate heating, poor plumbing characterize poor housing. Homelessness is largely attributable to lack of housing. Urban renewal programs often fail to help relocate displaced slum dwellers.
    D. Social class effects a person's likelihood of being arrested, indicted, convicted, and imprisoned. It also effects a youth's chances for being labeled delinquent. Affluent persons can usually gain release before trials and hire private attorneys.
V. Explanations of Persistent Poverty
    A. Structural explanations incorporate elements of both functionalist and conflict theory. Poverty is attributed to changes in institutions and conflicts between groups in response to these changes.
       1. Marxian views address problems of industrial workers in terms of loss of function due to automation and the removal of factories to third world countries.
       2. Structural arguments also address the establishment of a dual labor market.
       3. Radical structuralists argue that the state's welfare programs perpetuate poverty. Conservatives argue that welfare programs are too liberal.
    B. Cultural approaches explain poverty by attributing it to elements in the way of life among the poor. "Culture of poverty" theorists believe that extended periods of economic deprivation contribute to the development of new values and attitudes that are perpetuated among the impoverished. One aspect of this culture is a feeling of resignation and fatalism.
       1. The situational approach sees the behavior of the poor as an adaptive mechanism towards specific elements of the environment.
       2. Gans developed a cultural-situational approach in which structural elements causing people to feel there is no choice for them are examined.

3. Adaptation approaches view lower class culture as an adaptation to relative deprivation.
   4. Value-stretch approaches view the impoverished as holding two sets of values simultaneously.
VI. Social Policy
   A. Current social-welfare programs consist of few categories of aid:
      1. Human resource development programs which provide education, training, and/or skills development.
      2. Social insurance programs which compensate for income loss, regardless of income level.
      3. Cash income support programs for unemployable people.
      4. Income-in-kind programs which provide services.
   B. The Reagan administration holds a conservative attitude towards domestic social programs. It holds that there should be a "safety net" for the "deserving" poor. Drastic cuts in social-welfare spending were made by the administration.
   C. Many Americans fear welfare payments encourage dependency and discourage motivation. Countries that rely the least on welfare have strong employment policies.
   D. Single mothers have special problems particularly in relation to providing care for their children while they work. Part-time work, and the provision of adequate daycare, appear to be strategies to address this problem.
   E. Poor people's movements have developed in the U.S., especially in the 1960s and 1970s. Many of these agitated for greater local representation in policy and program development.

Key Terms:
Welfare State: a significant portion of the gross national product is taken by the state to provide minimum levels of social welfare for the poor, the aged, and the disabled.
New Deal: F.D. Roosevelt's policies for domestic social programs.
Great Society: L. B. Johnson's policies for domestic social programs.
Wealthfare: government programs and/or legislation which aids the rich in their accumulation of wealth.
Social Class: a large number of people with the same economic level of well-being.
Social Stratification: the different position of people in the social order with varying degrees of access to desirable goods and services.
Class stratification: differential grouping of people according to access to occupations, incomes, and skills.

Lumpenproletariat: a term defined by K. Marx as people marginal to society; they either dropped out of society or were never in it.

Dual Labor Market: favored groups gain access to better jobs while minorities are directed to a segment of the labor market with poorly paid, low security jobs.

Practice Test:

Multiple Choice Questions: Select the one best answer for each question below.

1. In which of the following areas are the poor NOT at a disadvantage:
   a. education
   b. housing
   c. healthcare
   d. none of the above.

2. Who was the first president to institute policies that promoted the welfare state:
   a. F. D. Roosevelt
   b. Hoover
   c. Eisenhower
   d. Johnson.

3. Which of the following statements is true:
   a. there has been a substantial increase, in the past 20 years, of wealthy citizens
   b. wealthy citizens have legitimate means to avoid paying taxes
   c. the U.S. is not considered to possess a welfare state
   d. none of the above.

4. Which of the following statements is NOT true:
   a. the poor want to work, and often do
   b. minority workers are more likely to be unemployed
   c. minority income differences are NOT found between minority and white educated workers
   d. the number of poor is expected to increase in the near future.

5. Social class in the U.S. is:
   a. viewed just in terms of income
   b. has both an objective and subjective dimension
   c. can be seen to be divided into two classes only
   d. none of the above.

6. Which of the following black/white comparisons are true:
   a. the gap between black and white educational levels has narrowed in the past 15 years
   b. black income is almost equivalent to white income
   c. black women are less likely than white women to head households
   d. racial discrimination in employment no longer exists.

7. Which of the following statements is **NOT** true:
   a. many migrant workers are rural poor
   b. many Native Americans are rural poor
   c. rural education is equivalent to urban education
   d. rural areas tend to have inadequate healthcare.
8. Which of the following statements regarding **welfare** recipients is **NOT** true:
   a. more than half of the children are legitimate
   b. women stay on welfare an average of 5 years or more
   c. welfare payments are, in most states, below the poverty level
   d. average families have less than three children.
9. The working poor:
   a. share in the American work ethic
   b. often are victims of calamities
   c. often work full-time but at minimum wages
   d. all of the above.
10. Which of the following statements concerning education programs is NOT true:
    a. pre-school programs decrease drop out rates
    b. pre-school programs decrease the need for special education
    c. teachers treat poor and middle class children the same way
    d. poor children often are in overcrowded classes.
11. Structural arguments to explain poverty include all of the following **EXCEPT**:
    a. people do not feel motivated to work
    b. the establishment of a dual labor market
    c. the welfare system itself perpetuates poverty
    d. some people are systematically discriminated against as a group.
12. Culture of poverty theory suggests that poverty:
    a. is a reaction to specific circumstances
    b. becomes perpetuated by values and attitudes that support it
    c. lies in structural problems of advanced capitalism
    d. is easily eradicated by work programs.
13. Which of the following views appears to fault poor people the most for their poverty:
    a. Marxian view
    b. Structural views
    c. culture of poverty
    d. situational approach.
14. Which type of program incorporates welfare subsidies:
    a. cash support programs
    b. social-insurance programs
    c. human resource development
    d. income-in-kind services.
15. The Reagan administration's social-welfare policy:

a. expanded domestic welfare programs
  b. reduced domestic welfare programs
  c. substituted national health insurance for medicaid
  d. highlighted the need to create more comprehensive programs.
16. Which of the following has been advanced as a means of reducing poverty:
  a. increase worker's wages
  b. provide greater earned income tax credit for the poor
  c. develop more government sponsored work programs
  d. all of the above.

Essay Questions:
1. Explain the assertion in the text that equality of opportunity is basic to American ideals but the equality of outcome is not.
2. It has been asserted that the U.S. has the means to eradicate poverty. Why do you think such a goal has not been accomplished?
3. Describe and contrast structural and cultural theories of poverty.
4. What social policies would you develop to eradicate poverty?

Test Answers:
Multiple Choice:
1. d
2. a
3. b
4. c
5. b
6. a
7. c
8. b
9. d
10. c
11. a
12. b
13. c
14. a
15. b
16. d

Essay Questions:
Answers should address the following issues:
1. Equality is an ideal impeded by discriminatory practices.
   - Attitudes suggest that the poor deserve to be so because they are lazy.
   - Attitudes also suggest that the rich are entitled to their material wealth.
2. Poverty is perpetuated by structural discrimination.
   - Poverty eradication is not reflected on the government's budget priorities (which favor military and defense spending).
   - Work in the U.S. is often low paid and devoid of benefits such as health insurance.
   - Attitudes towards the poor mitigate against developing policies to eradicate poverty.
3. Basically, structural views would support changing structures and institutions in the society.
   - Cultural views advocate changing people's attitudes and implicitly blame the poor person rather than looking at discrimination and other structural impediments.
4. Essentially reversing the patterns discussed in question 2, above.

CHAPTER NINE: PREJUDICE AND DISCRIMINATION

Chapter Summary:
   The chapter begins with a brief historical review of constitutional amendments and legislative programs geared to the reduction of discrimination. The nature of minority group status is reviewed. The mechanisms of prejudice and discrimination are also presented. Special attention is paid to institutional discrimination as a structural means of perpetuating discrimination. Discrimination in the institutions of housing, education, occupations, and the justice system are reviewed.
   The psychological and social consequences of prejudice and discrimination are also addressed. Social policy issues relating to prejudice and discrimination are presented. Special attention is focused on the role of government, affirmative action programs, and schooling policy.

Learning Objectives:
   After studying the chapter the student should be able:
   - to understand the development of the laws and policies which were designed to promote equality.
   - to elaborate the meaning and definition of a minority group.
   - to explain the meaning and nature of prejudice and discrimination.
   - to explain the form and nature of institutional discrimination, particularly in the economy; workplace; education; housing.
   - to identify the effects of prejudice and discrimination, especially on the recipients.
   - to address social policy issues in the area of prejudice and discrimination.

Chapter Outline:
I. Prejudice and Discrimination
   A. The constitutional basis for equality was laid in the 1860s and 1870s with the 13th, 14th, and 15th amendments. These rights did not begin to be effective until the mid-twentieth century.
      1. A major legal breakthrough occurred in 1954 with the Brown v. Bd. of Education Supreme Court decision. This ruling established separate educational institutions as inherently illegal.
      2. Voting Rights Act of 1965 and The Civil Rights Act of 1968 also aided in the struggle for equality.
      3. A 1967 government commission established to investigate racial riots found that the society was headed towards two separate and unequal societies, one black and one white.

  B. Small immigrant groups seem better able to adjust to their new environment in the U.S. Larger groups experience more difficulty, particularly competing in the general labor market.
II. The Meaning of "Minority"
  A. There are racial and ethnic minority groups in the U.S. Minority groups share characteristics, such as subordination to a dominant group; undesirable characteristics; an in-group or "we-feeling;" group membership through being born into the group; and tendency to practice endogamy. Minority groups are not necessarily smaller in numbers. As they assimilate, they lose some of their distinct characteristics.
III. Defining Prejudice and Discrimination
  A. Discrimination, or behavior that treats people differently according to their group membership, is different from prejudice. Prejudice is attitudes that are emotional, preconceived, categorical perceptions of others. A person can be discriminatory without being prejudiced, and vice versa.
IV. Origins of Prejudice and Discrimination
  A. Psychological approaches include "scapegoating" or displacing aggression onto a source other than the one that generated it. These feelings can be generalized to a whole group. Projection, displacing one's own negative characteristics onto others, also is a psychological explanation.
  B. Discrimination can take many forms including practical or symbolic acts. Economic exploitation is one type of overt discrimination. Jim Crow laws were often of a symbolic nature.
  C. Prejudice may be part of the social learning of norms passed from one generation to another. Stereotyping is another way people learn prejudice.
V. Institutional Discrimination (ID)
  A. ID is the unconscious result of the structure and functioning of institutions and policies.
  B. Problems dealt with in terms of educational institutions today address how to achieve racial integration; how and what makes quality education; the question of tax support for private schools. Education is perceived as the means of social and economic advancement. The gap between blacks and whites in educational attainment is narrowing. Minority group members, at all educational levels, earn less than their counterparts.
  C. The manner and effects of school desegregation is a much debated issue today. There does appear to be advantages for minority students as a result of busing for integration. "White flight" or the moving of whites outside of urban school districts, has impeded school

integration.
   1. Opponents of busing feel it takes away funds that could be utilized for instruction. They also feel it hinders local control of schools. Proponents of busing point to studies that show black students who attend integrated schools achieve more and are more likely to attend integrated universities and live and work in integrated communities. The effects on desegregation and quality of education are inconclusive but appear to suggest improvements.
   D. Housing segregation has increased in the last few decades. Whites have moved increasingly to suburbs while blacks have moved to cities. A 1965 court ruling prohibits discrimination in the sale, rental, or financing of suburban housing. It has not been enforced. Real estate practices perpetuate housing discrimination.
   E. The American work ethic asserts that anyone who wants to work can. American attitudes usually also imply that the wealthy deserve to be so as do the poor. Union locals often have upheld discriminatory practices. Overall, minority group members hold a disproportionate amount of low level jobs. They are also paid less for the same jobs. The employment gap between whites and Hispanic and black groups has widened.
   F. Discrimination plagues the criminal justice system in all areas from arrest, detainment, disposition, sentencing, bail practices.
VI. Consequences of Prejudice and Discrimination
   A. Prejudice and discrimination effect an individual's personality characteristics. Friendly contact between children of different races changes attitudes towards the other race.
   B. Beginning in the 1950s, after the success of the Montgomery bus boycott, broad social movements for desegregation developed.
VII. Social Policy
   A. Policy in the 1960s focused on aiding in the training and placement of unemployed workers. Programs often were too small and underfunded to adequately address the need. The Reagan administration worsened the situation by looking to private industry to take up the slack in cuts in government work programs. Government programs often do not adequately address market needs and are often not adequately financed.
   B. Affirmative action programs were an out growth of the 1964 Civil Rights Act. Their goals are aided by the Equal Employment Opportunity Commission.
   C. Perhaps the best way to attain school desegregation would be through urban/suburban busing. This does not

happen because they are in different school districts.
D. Head Start programs often have beneficial effects but some critics feel it is too little, too late.
E. The 1990s is projected to be a difficult decade in which minorities will have to fight to retain recent gains. Federal budgets will probably shrink, decreasing jobs in the public sector. Minority employment in the private sector has been more difficult than government employment.

Key Terms:
Oriental Exclusion: the attempt to keep Asians from the U.S. or from local labor markets to reduce competition for jobs.
Racial Minorities: groups of people who share inherited characteristics.
Ethnic Minorities: groups of people who share cultural characteristics such as national origin, religion, language, a common history.
Minority Group: members of a group that are subordinated to another more powerful group; often seen as possessing inferior or undesirable characteristics.
Endogamy: marrying within a group having similar characteristics.
Assimilation: taking on the values, attitudes, and characteristics of the dominant group.
Discrimination: the differential treatment of persons due to their social group membership.
Ethnocentric: the tendency to see one's own behavioral patterns and belief structures as desirable and natural.
Prejudice: emotional attitudes which cause a person to see others in a categorical, predetermined way.
Scapegoat: the displacing of aggression onto a source other than the one that provoked it.
Projection: displacing one's own negative characteristics onto others.
Social Norm: a social standard that specifies behavior appropriate to a situation.
Stereotyping: attributing a fixed and usually unfavorable or inaccurate conception to a group of people.
Institutional Discrimination: discrimination built into the structure of society.
De Jure Segregation: segregation required by law.
De Facto Segregation: segregation that stems from practices such as segregated neighborhoods.
Blockbusting: selling houses to minorities at inflated prices.
Racial Steering: the refusal of real estate agents to show houses to minorities that are outside of certain neighborhoods.

Affirmative Action: programs which seek to compensate for institutional discrimination by increasing opportunities for minorities.

Head Start: programs aimed at preparing disadvantaged children for school.

Practice Test:

Multiple Choice Questions:
select the best answer for each question below.
1. Effective moves towards enforcing racial equality first began in:
   a. the 1860s
   b. the turn of the century
   c. the 1920s
   d. the 1950s.
2. Which of the following is **NOT** a characteristic of a minority group:
   a. they are subordinate
   b. they are smaller
   c. they lose their distinctiveness in assimilation
   d. their perceived characteristics are devalued.
3. The belief that blacks are intellectually inferior is an example of:
   a. prejudice
   b. discrimination
   c. ethnocentrism
   d. none of the above.
4. "Women are too emotional" is an example of:
   a. projection
   b. stereotyping
   c. scapegoating
   d. discrimination.
5. In the U.S. today, you are most likely to see:
   a. full racial integration
   b. de jure segregation
   c. de facto segregation
   d. none of the above.
6. Racial desegregation in schools:
   a. appears to have no effects
   b. appears to help the minority students
   c. is aided by white flight
   d. is more common in the suburbs.
7. Housing segregation and discrimination in the U.S.:
   a. has increased in the last few decades
   b. is aided by real estate agent practices
   c. is actually prohibited by law
   d. all of the above.
8. Employment of minorities:
   a. has not been equivalent to educational gains
   b. is similar to whites in types of jobs

c. is paid equally to whites for the same job
   d. none of the above.
9. Bail practices are determined:
   a. by a person's ability to pay ✓
   b. by a group of peers
   c. equitably for all groups
   d. are no longer utilized.
10. Racial prejudice today:
    a. is no longer found
    b. is never directed towards successful minorities
    c. can be unlearned by exposure to other groups ✓
    d. exists only against blacks and Hispanics.
11. Government programming with regard to work training programs:
    a. are generally underfunded and inadequate when they do exist
    b. was cut by the Reagan administration
    c. was supposed to be compensated for by tax credits to private industry
    d. all of the above. ✓
12. Affirmative Action programs are geared towards:
    a. the establishment of absolute quotas
    b. the extension of opportunities to past victims of discrimination ✓
    c. were boosted by the 1984 Firefighters Local union case
    d. all of the above.
13. Parents whose children have actually been bused demonstrate more favorable attitudes towards busing than parents whose children have not been bused.
    a. true ✓
    b. false
14. Which of the following statements about Head Start programs is **NOT** true:
    a. they are federally funded programs
    b. they provide jobs for adults in the community
    c. they do not seem to have any psychological benefits for the children ✓
    d. they do appear to promote intellectual achievement.
15. Which factor is predicted to impede minority living in the 1990s:
    a. the reduction of government jobs ✓
    b. increased white migration to the cities
    c. more liberal attitudes in government spending
    d. all of the above.

Essay Questions:
1. Why do you think prejudice and discrimination persist in contemporary society?
2. What do you think should be essential to changing the segregation of public schools and the equalization of edu-

cation in general?
3. How would you address the overall situation of prejudice and discrimination in the U.S.?

Test Answers:
Multiple Choice:
1. d
2. b
3. a
4. b
5. c
6. b
7. d
8. a
9. a
10. c
11. d
12. b
13. a
14. c
15. a

Essay Questions:
The student should address the following issues:
1. Address issues of the social learning of prejudiced attitudes.
 - Lack of integration of neighborhoods and schools perpetuates isolation of the racial groups.
 - Lack of exposure perpetuates prejudice.
 - Deal with issues of institutional racism and the perpetuation of especially educational and occupational discrimination.
2. Here the issue of desegregating neighborhoods needs to be dealt with.
 - The issue of suburban vs. urban populations is also essential. How will these become integrated?
 - Development of stronger funding for daycare and better pre-school programs would also seem to be a step in creating better overall education.
3. Issues concerning the economic situation of many minorities are essential to address.
 - Stronger housing integration enforcement would also help to change other opportunities, including the unlearning of prejudice.
 - Fuller, more comprehensive government sponsored work programs could provide decent wages for minority persons having difficulty finding employment.

CHAPTER TEN: SEX ROLES AND INEQUALITY

Chapter Summary:
The chapter begins with a discussion of the inequalities which exist in the U.S. between the sexes. The traditional sex roles which influence most males and females are presented. The nature and areas of sexism in society are reviewed, particularly in terms of women's role as homemaker. The manner of socialization, education, psychiatry, and the media in perpetuating sex stereotyping and discrimination is reviewed. Finally, social policy options to address these areas are presented.

Learning Objectives:
After studying the chapter, the student should be able:
- to describe the inequality between the sexes as it exists in the U.S.
- to delineate the nature and content of traditional sex roles.
- to explain the nature and forms of sexism in the U.S. (against both men and women).
- to elaborate the source and perpetuation of sex roles and sexism.
- to review social policy issues in regard to sex roles and sexism.

Chapter Outline:
I. Sex Roles and Inequality
    A. In the past twenty years women have made some notable gains. Women's participation in male-dominated professions has increased. By 1988, the median income of full-time working women was 68% of men's; up from 62% in 1979. Still, 59% of working women work in the "girl's ghetto," and women earn less than men in the same occupations. The Equal Rights Amendment (ERA) failed to be ratified by 38 states and also did not receive a 2/3's majority in the House of Representatives.
II. Traditional Sex Roles
    A. Until recently women's expected roles were that of wife, mother, and homemaker. A man was expected to be a leader and provider. Women were considered too frail to take men's roles. Men were expected to "act like a man," and to be dominant and unemotional.
    B. Resistance to change in traditional sex roles is strong. Anti-ERA opposition stemmed partially from women who felt it threatened their identities or lifestyles.
    C. Sex-role learning begins early in life. Often this learning reinforces aggression in boys and passivity in

girls.
III. The Nature of Sexism
   A. Traditional sex role characteristics of women include passivity, domesticity, and envy. Male sex-typing includes images of men as tough, dominant, and unemotional. Many people victimized by stereotypes nevertheless adhere to them. Stereotypic images of women, held by men, significantly impede their progress.
   B. Women are concentrated in lower-status jobs at the end of the pay scale. Work that is traditionally done by women often is significantly paid at lower wages than comparable work done by men.
   C. Women's role at home is not valued in the market place. This is reflected in women's inability to get disability, to establish credit, not received tax credit for homemaking, and other means of discrimination against women who do not work outside the home.
   D. The women's movement dates back to the suffrage movement to gain the vote. Renewal of interest was promoted by the civil rights movement of the 1960s. The 1964 Civil Rights Act included the prohibition of discrimination against women in employment. In 1966 the National Organization of Women was formed to promote women's rights. By the late 1970s and early 1980s, opposition to the women's movement increased and progress slowed.
IV. Sources of Sexism
   A. Socialization in the family, education, media, and language plays a large part in forming sexist attitudes.
   B. Schools reinforce traditional sex roles. Teachers demonstrate different attitudes towards, and expectations of, girls and boys.
   C. Traditional family roles devalue the importance of homemaking. Evidence in research on nontraditional marriages indicates that the male's profession is more highly valued. The motherhood role is so highly valued that women with grown children, especially among women who do not work, have a strong tendency to be depressed.
   D. In psychiatry traditional sex role biases can effect the therapeutic relationship.
   E. The media, especially in advertisements, perpetuates images of women as sex objects. Sexism often is perpetuated by the language itself.
   F. Although women are more active in church related activities, they are unlikely to be in leadership roles. Only very recently have some of the more liberal denominations admitted women to the clergy.

G. The federal government has a long history of
   discrimination against women in its living practices.
   State labor laws are differentially enforced with regard to sex. Women suffer a great deal of harassment
   on the job. Men suffer more discrimination in family
   law.
V. Social Policy
   A. Changes in child-rearing practices are advocated.
   There is evidence that young children need a consistent
   relationship with an adult. There is no evidence that
   this needs to be the mother. Efforts to promote more
   equal parenting include better maternity leaves; pater-
   nity leaves; benefits for part-time work; better childcare; sharing of household chores.
   B. Changes in education are advanced to promote
   equality. These include more sensitivity to stereotyping; equal treatment of both sexes; more male ele-
   mentary school teachers; changes in the curriculum;
   better vocational guidance.
   C. Women are discriminated against in the criminal
   justice system. Although comparable worth programs
   have received little overall support, isolated cases of
   sex discrimination have been favorably resolved. In
   1988, a large claim against the State Farm Insurance
   Company was settled in the women's favor.
   D. Reproductive control, and liberal abortion laws are
   a large area of controversy. Legalized abortions have
   dropped the rate of mortality and injury. Issues of
   sex education and contraception are hotly debated,
   particularly in relation to the role of public schools.
   E. The women's movement will probably focus its attention on the problems of single parent households and
   low-income families. Childcare and children's aid are
   current concerns in the women's movement.
   F. Men are agitating against male stereotypes.
   Women's roles in the workforce will have an effect on
   men's participation and competition.

Key Terms:
Girl's Ghetto: traditionally female occupations such as re-
   tail sales; insurance; real estate; and service
   occupations (telephone operators, clerks, secretaries,
   receptionists).
Gender Identity: a person's identification with the role
   and characteristics of masculine or feminine (as distinct from biological sex).
Sexism: attitudes, behaviors, laws, and traditions that
   discriminate against an individual on the basis of her
   or his gender.
Comparable Worth: adjusting payment for jobs to reflect the

intrinsic value of the job.
NOW: The National Organization of Women, founded in 1966, to promote the rights of women to equality in all aspects of life.
Socialization: the process by which humans become social beings.

Practice Test:
Multiple Choice Questions: Select the best answer for each question below.
1. In 1988, the median income earned by full-time working women was _____ percent of men's earned income.
    a. 50
    b. 55
    c. 59
    ⓓ. 68
2. The majority of women in the U.S.:
    a. don't work
    ⓑ. work in the "girl's ghetto" occupations
    c. work in the professions
    d. none of the above.
3. The Equal Rights Amendment:
    a. passed in 1982
    b. passed in 1983
    ⓒ. has never been passed
    d. is not promoted by women's rights activists.
4. Which of the following is **NOT** true:
    a. men are not expected to be domestic
    b. women appear to avoid professional issues
    ⓒ. work in a job is valued equally no matter who does it
    d. none of the above.
5. Comparable worth programs:
    a. address inequities of "women's work" payment
    b. are contested as too expensive
    c. would somewhat correct the gender earnings gap
    ⓓ. all of the above.
6. The women's movement in the U.S. <u>initially</u> began:
    a. to free the slaves
    ⓑ. to win the vote
    c. to gain access to men's occupations
    d. to gain comparable worth.
7. Women's rights activists agitate for all of the following **EXCEPT**:
    a. government subsidized daycare
    ⓑ. stricter abortion laws
    c. the ERA
    d. maternity leaves.
8. Which of the following areas is **NOT** a major source of sex role learning:

72

a. parents
   b. school
   c. television
   d. none of the above.
9. Which of the following does **NOT** occur in most educational settings:
   a. school books which focus on boys and men
   b. girls portrayed in occupational roles in textbooks
   c. sex differentiation in vocational counseling
   d. different behavioral standards for boys and girls.
10. Which of the following statements about married women is **NOT** true:
    a. working wives are less depressed than housewives
    b. women are more satisfied in marriage than husbands
    c. even in happy marriages women are less satisfied than men
    d. none of the above.
11. Which of the following statements about women and religion is **NOT** true:
    a. There are no women clergy in the U.S.
    b. women are more active in church activities
    c. God is always referred to as "He" in traditional denominations and religions
    d. the major western religions devalue women.
12. In which area are men more likely to suffer discrimination:
    a. in the federal government
    b. in academic settings
    c. in family court
    d. none of the above.
13. Which of the following is **NOT** promoted to help fathers become more active parents:
    a. benefits paid to part-time workers
    b. better maternity and paternity leaves
    c. more quality daycare
    d. none of the above.
14. A 1984 Supreme Court ruling in <u>Grove City College v. Bell</u> established:
    a. equal funding of all sports in higher education
    b. affirmative action programs in professional schools
    c. nondiscrimination in education is applied only to programs receiving federal aid (not to institutions)
    d. none of the above.

Essay Questions:
1. Why do you think sex discrimination is to persistent in society?
2. How do you feel about traditional sex roles? Are they positive or negative? Explain your response.

3. If you believe sex discrimination is bad, how would **you** develop strategies to combat it?

Test Answers:
Multiple Choice:
1. d
2. b
3. c
4. c
5. d
6. b
7. b
8. d
9. b
10. c
11. a
12. c
13. d
14. c

Essay Questions:
The student should address the following issues:
1. Socialization and sex role learning in the family.
   - Discrimination in behavior and attitudes in educational institutions.
   - People's resistance to changing characteristics in which they are emotionally invested.
   - Economic discrimination which mitigates against women's independence.
2. Issues of women's difficulty in the work and economic spheres.
   - Issues of discrimination against men as parents and/or homemakers.
   - Issues of the psychological value and detriment of sex-typing.
3. Develop different work structures: better part-time opportunities, leave options, flexitime.
   - Change educational materials.
   - Require educators to integrate women/girls more in teaching and materials.
   - Encourage parents to participate more equally in child-rearing.

CHAPTER ELEVEN: AN AGING SOCIETY

Chapter Summary:
Industrial societies include a larger proportion of elderly than earlier societies. The marginalization of the elderly in contemporary society also appears to be unique to industrial societies. The consequences of a "roleless role" for the elderly are presented.

Technological and scientific advances have promoted the growth of the elderly population. Ageist attitudes and practices pervade the society. These are reviewed and the facts about the aging process are presented. Problems the elderly face with respect to poverty, health care, isolation, and family life are discussed.

The special problems the elderly face with regard to retirement and the proximity of death are examined. Potential ways of dealing with these, and other issues facing the elderly, are dealt with in the final section of social policy.

Learning Objectives:
After studying the chapter the student should be able:
- to identify industrial societies as having large populations of elderly and relegating them to the margins of society.
- to explain the sociological perspectives' views of the elderly problem.
- to elaborate the sources and forms of ageism.
- to describe the aging process.
- to address some of the problems accompanying the aging of the population, particularly in terms of economic, family, and health care pressures.
- to explain the views and research in the area of death and dying.
- to elaborate social policy issues effecting the elderly.

Chapter Outline:
I. An Aging Society
   A. Industrialized societies have a greater proportion of elderly than other societies. Infant mortality rates, fertility rates, and life expectancy contribute to the age of the population. In the U.S., many elderly feel relegated to a "roleless role." Problems with the elderly concern their labeling, loss of the work role, and economic deprivation. The average income of the elderly has improved in the last several decades.
II. Perspectives on Aging
   A. Functionalists view problems of the aged in terms

of the failure of institutions to fulfill their needs adequately. Interactionists focus on the stigma, prejudice, and discrimination to which the elderly are exposed.

III. American Elderly Today
   A. Technological and scientific advances have improved the infant mortality rate and provided cures for previously fatal diseases. Forced retirement has occurred to remove elderly workers and give young workers opportunities.
   B. Age stratification segregates the elderly. By isolating the aged it promotes disengagement and retreat. The aged population has tripled since 1980 and is continuing to increase. Two-thirds of the elderly are urban residents. The elderly also comprise the largest proportion of the population of small towns.
   C. Federal laws passed in 1967 and 1976 protect workers between the ages of 40-70 years from discrimination. Little is done to enforce these laws and people over the age of 70 years are not included in the law. The aged are also discriminated against by the government, the media, the medical community, and a society that overemphasizes youth.
   D. The elderly have low status and negative images in society. The elderly have a higher than average suicide rate. This is attributed largely to isolation and an absence of external social restraints.

IV. Dimensions of the Aging Process
   A. Chronological aging is an automatic process. Aspects of physical health degenerate over time. Most significantly, is a decline in the body's immune defense system. Body systems degenerate at different rates. Older people are more susceptible to stress. At the same time, stress can be an agent of secondary aging.
   B. The aged are in contracting social situations and in new, poorly defined roles. Negative stereotypes pervade the image of the elderly. Loss of economic productivity is also psychologically difficult. The isolation of the aged promotes dependency on negative social images of the elderly. The elderly suffer decreases in self-esteem as a result.
   C. The intellectual capacity of most elderly remain unimpaired until extreme old age. Often the psychological depression suffered by the elderly is mistaken for senility.
   D. The aged constitute a minority in that they are subject to prejudice, stereotyping, and discrimination. Actually, the aged are a significant

political force because of their increasing numbers and their high voter rates.
    E. Older women become devalued earlier than men. This is associated with overall societal views of women. Contrary to stereotypes of elderly women:
        1. they go to doctors, on the whole, less than younger people;
        2. widowed women have a strong sense of personal identity;
        3. older women's activities do not differ appreciably from men's or from people in middle age;
        4. elderly women, and men, still express interest and activity in the area of sexuality.

V. Concomitants of Aging
    A. The elderly do not particularly perceive themselves as victims of violent crime.
    B. The elderly are prone to high health care costs. Medicare covers only half of physician expenditures. Only 2/3s of the elderly have private health insurance. Thirty-five percent of medicaid expenditures go to elderly care.
    C. Economic discrimination occurs not only through mandatory retirement but through overall discrimination against older workers.
        1. Old people who are women and/or minority group members face multiple economic hazards.
    D. Stresses can be felt in the family due to an aged parent or grandparent. Twenty-five percent of the elderly live with one of their children. Distance between families and the divorce rate mitigate against providing elderly care in the home.

VI. Retirement
    A. Proponents of mandatory retirement feel that it helps make space for younger workers, aids affirmative action programs, and helps plans for the future by setting a target date. Opponents believe that retirement is discriminatory, detrimental to health, strains the social security system, and promotes poverty. It is unclear whether most workers would prefer to keep working or not.
    B. Many retirees lack role models and reference groups. Difficulties with retirement concerned the loss of income, missing work, and fears about the health or loss of a spouse. The greatest difficulty with retirement was found among people whose greatest satisfaction came from work.

VII. Death
    A. The U.S., as a whole, has a fear of death and an inability to deal with dying as a natural process. Research indicates the aged have less fear of death

than the young. E. Kubler-Ross elaborated stages that people go through in the grieving process.

VIII. Social Policy
A. The majority of the elderly live in family settings. The percentage of elderly living alone is rapidly increasing. Most elderly express a preference for living in some independent manner; most are averse to group living.
B. Medicare is in financial trouble due to the great increase in the proportion of elderly in the population. Suggestions to revamp the Medicare benefit system have been made. Additionally, suggestions concerning preventive measures and cost containment have been advanced.
C. Social security has become the main income source for many elderly. The system has been criticized because low-income workers pay a greater proportion of social security taxes and often rely completely on social security in old age. Other criticisms of the program hold that it discriminates against women; does not effect nonwage income; and, it penalizes elderly workers.

Key Terms:
Roleless Role: the tendency for the aged to be relegated to vague roles on the fringe of society.
Age Stratification: the segregation of people according to their ages.
Young-Old: people 65-75 years of age.
Old-Old: people over 75 years of age.
Ageism: bias, prejudice, and discrimination towards people on the basis of age.
Gerontology: the study and practice of the aging process and its causes.
Primary Aging: molecular and cellular changes.
Secondary Aging: an acceleration of normal aging caused by environmental factors.
Senility: the loss of intellectual and cognitive functioning in some elderly.
Hospices: institutions that aid people in the process of dying.

Practice Test:
Multiple Choice Questions: select the best answer for each question below.
1. Which of the following is NOT generally a problem of the elderly:
   a. loss of intellectual ability
   b. loss of work role

c. economic deprivation
d. labeled by stereotypic thinking.

2. Age discrimination for workers aged 40-70 was passed in:
a. 1920
b. 1944
c. 1976
d. 1988.

3. Television and other media:
a. spend a lot of money addressing elderly issues
b. often show a negative view of aging and the elderly
c. depict the elderly as sexual beings
d. none of the above.

4. Which group has the highest suicide rates:
a. widowed men
b. widowed women
c. married elderly
d. never married elderly

5. The most significant health risk <u>generally</u> in the aged population is:
a. acute illness
b. loss of organ functions
c. decrease in immune deficiencies
d. skin degeneration.

6. Negative psychological factors include all of the following EXCEPT:
a. loss of economic productivity
b. contracting social situation
c. negative labeling by society
d. none of the above.

7. Senility in the aged:
a. is common by age 70
b. often is actually depression
c. never is associated with age
d. none of the above.

8. Which of the following is true about elderly women:
a. they go to the doctor more frequently than men
b. they are not interested in sex
c. if widowed they maintain no self-identity
d. they are no less active than men or middle-aged women.

9. <u>Opponents</u> of mandatory retirement feel it does all of the following EXCEPT:
a. helps affirmative action
b. promotes discrimination
c. strains the social security system
d. promotes poverty.

10. White of the following was not a negative aspect of retirement:

    a. reduced income
    b. missing one's job
    c. emphasis on personal relations
    d. inflexibility.
11. Which of the following activities is most common among the elderly to date:
    a. television viewing
    b. reading
    c. gardening
    d. all of the above.
12. Old people experience less fear of death than do young people:
    a. true
    b. false.
13. Which of the following living situations among the elderly is increasing the most:
    a. nursing homes
    b. living with children
    c. living alone
    d. living with a spouse.

Essay Questions:
1. Why do ageist attitudes persist and what can be done about them?
2. Do you think that mandatory retirement should be legal or not? Explain.
3. If you were a politician or legislator, how would you address the problems of the elderly?

Test Answers:
Multiple Choice:
1. a
2. c
3. b
4. a
5. c
6. d
7. b
8. d
9. a
10. c
11. a
12. a
13. c

Essay Questions:
1. Age segregation and lack of exposure between generations should be addressed.
- The marginalization of the elderly from social relations and work is also important.
- The confounding of depression, as a result of the elderly's experiences, should be viewed in terms of alternative roles for the elderly.
2. Issues of discrimination; personal rights; unemployment among the young; poverty among the old; the inadequacy of Medicare and social security should be dealt with.
3. Relevant policy issues include: the modification of the social security system; the provision of adequate income, health care, and housing; the usefulness and content of elderly roles; the incorporation of elderly concerns and preferences.

CHAPTER TWELVE: THE CHANGING FAMILY

Chapter Summary:
   The chapter begins with a discussion of whether the family unit in the U.S. is in crisis or just adapting to societal changes. The nature and characteristics of modern nuclear family life in the U.S. is explored. The pressures exerted by increased employment among married women with children is addressed. Pressures of single-parent families and impoverished families are also viewed.
   Social problems effecting the family are also presented. These include problems associated with divorce, illegitimate children, poverty, and technological advances such as surrogate motherhood. Social policies promoted to aid the stability and well-being of the family are examined. Comprehensive family support in the community appears to help many family problems.

Learning Objectives:
   After studying the chapter the student should be able:
   - to identify the concern with the family as the source of many social problems and the debate about whether or not the family is breaking down.
   - to address changes in family size, function, and roles in the recent past, particularly issues of women working, childlessness, and single parenting.
   - to elaborate the social problems afflicting today's families; particularly divorce, illegitimacy, homelessness/poverty, and surrogacy.
   - to discuss social policy areas at issue in the area of family life.

Chapter Outline:
I.   The Changing Family
     A. There has been much discussion in the past several decades concerning the crisis of the family. Some argue the family is breaking down while others believe it is undergoing constructive reorganization. Nevertheless, the family is singled out as the source of many social problems.
II. The Nature of the Family
     A. The nuclear family is most likely to be found in hunting and gathering societies and in industrial societies. Extended families are more likely to be in agrarian societies. Industrial societies favor small units because of geographic mobility and the fact that children do not work.
     B. Families undergo changes in the roles of family members. Members need to know and meet role expectations. Family roles need to meet societal needs as

well as individual psychological needs. The family must also be adaptive to change.

C. Sometimes marriages are held together by external pressures rather than by desire. Economic pressures and habit and fear of change contribute to this.

D. By 1988, only 28% of U.S. families fit the traditional model of worker/father, homemaker/mother, and children. Over 60% of women with children work outside the home. Many attribute family problems to women working outside the home. Certainly, traditional male and female roles have become modified.

   1. A woman's employment outside the home has been viewed as detrimental to marriage, by some. Her economic independence makes her more likely to leave an unsatisfactory marriage.

   2. Part-time work is sought by women because often they maintain the bulk of household responsibilities. Part-time work, however, lacks security, benefits, and adequate pay.

E. The presence of children tends to decrease marital happiness and add stress. The happiest couples are young, childless ones. In 1986, the U.S. recorded its lowest fertility rate in its history. More couples are choosing to remain childless. These marriages appear to be more satisfying to the adults.

F. The poverty and discrimination that effects the black population are thought to influence the life of the family. A large proportion of black families are women-headed households, though this is associated with poverty; the majority of black families are stable and headed by men.

III. Divorce

A. As late as 1966, the divorce rate was 2.5. By 1988, it increased to 4.5 per 1000. One third of all divorces occur in the first three years.

B. Shrinking family size and function are factors in the divorce rate as is the increase in the tolerance of divorce.

C. Divorce is accompanied by great financial and emotional strain. Divorce is also extremely stressful in the effects it has on children, many of whom are young at the time the divorce occurs.

IV. Postponement of Marriage

A. Increasing age of marriage impacts to decrease family size, extended family size, and the number of childless couples.

V. Reproductive Issues

A. Social changes have caused technological changes which have influenced the technology as well. Amniocentsis, surrogacy, and other reproductive

innovations have become significant in recent years.
B. Illegitimacy and premarital pregnancies are not as stigmatized as they once were. The biggest problems associated with illegitimacy are problems also felt by other single parents. Much illegitimacy occurs among minor women.
C. Homelessness has been recognized as a problem since the early 1980s. Families at risk often are suffering from a crisis which dramatically reduces their income.

VI. Social Policy
A. Many promote change in the divorce laws, particularly in relation to eliminating the concept of fault. Critics feel that easy access will promote divorce.
   1. No-fault reforms have reduced alimony payments to women. Some believe this has resulted in unfair treatment of women.
   2. Only 61% of women not living with the father of their children were awarded support payments in 1986. Of these, only half received full payment.
B. Laws governing social security and property rights of illegitimate children are beginning to be modified to end discrimination against these children.
C. Various proposals have been advanced to aid families. These include:
   1. greater support to low-income families with two parents;
   2. the provision of parental leaves in the workplace;
   3. more government support for childcare services;
   4. more community and state aid for support services such as family centers.

Key Terms:
Kinship Unit: a group of individuals related by bloodlines or by some institution equivalent to marriage.
Nuclear Family: a father, mother, and their children living separately from other kin.
Extended Family: parents, children, grandchildren, aunts, uncles, and others living together.
Divorce Ratio: the number of divorced persons per 1000 married persons living with their spouses.
Marriage Squeeze: the number of women who would like to marry is greater than the number of available men.
Surrogacy: a women is artificially inseminated and gives up the child to its natural parent; she is normally paid a great deal for this.
Alimony: money paid, in a divorce, by one partner to support another.

Practice Test:

Multiple Choice Questions: Select the best answer for each question below.
1. Extended families are most likely to be found in:
   a. hunting and gathering societies
   b. industrial societies
   c. agrarian societies
   d. post-industrial societies.
2. Industrial societies favor the nuclear family because:
   a. it allows for geographic mobility
   b. it maintains large family size
   c. it is dependent on intergenerational support
   d. it is similar to agrarian families.
3. Which group of women is most satisfied in marriage, according to a study in the text:
   a. women who choose to stay home
   b. women who choose to work
   c. women who have to work
   d. none of the above.
4. A factor that some have felt contributes to divorce is:
   a. heightened male participation in the home
   b. women working in the labor force
   c. women's growing perception of lack of alternatives
   d. the availability of single men in middle-age.
5. The fertility rate in the U.S. has:
   a. has increased steadily since 1945
   b. has decreased steadily since 1945
   c. has remained constant in the 20th century
   d. hit an all-time low in 1986.
6. Much of the differences between black and white families can be attributed to:
   a. different values in life
   b. poverty
   c. different views of sex roles
   d. less desire to keep the family intact.
7. In the U.S. today:
   a. marriage does not appear to be a chosen form
   b. more couples divorce after a long marriage than after a short one
   c. the marriage rate has decreased in the past 20 years.
   d. there were half as many divorces, in recent years, as there were marriages.
8. Which of the following has NOT been advanced as a cause of divorce:
   a. growing community support services for single parents
   b. increased education and employment of women
   c. reformation of divorce laws

9.   d.   loss of functions fulfilled by the family unit.
9. The postponement of marriage to later ages results in:
   a. higher divorce rates
   b. earlier childbearing within the marriage
   c. a "marriage squeeze" for some women
   d. a smaller proportion of the population living along.
10. Critics of surrogacy suggest all of the following **EXCEPT**:
    a. it creates a broader class of women
    b. it is only an option for the affluent
    c. it is unethical given the availability of children for adoption
    d. it alleviates the distress of infertile couples.
11. Homeless families usually are:
    a. chronically and consistently homeless.
    b. a majority of the homeless population.
    c. suffering from a crisis situation.
    d. two-parent families.
12. Women suffer often in divorce because of:
    a. changes in alimony due to no-fault divorce
    b. lack of payment of child support money
    c. common-law property rulings
    d. all of the above.
13. What program has been effective in helping many problems from spouse abuse to teen pregnancy:
    a. welfare programs
    b. family planning agencies
    c. comprehensive family support programs
    d. income tax credits.

<u>Essay Questions</u>:
1. Do you think that the American family is an endangered species?
2. What do you see as the biggest problem in family life today?
3. What would you do to support the well-being of families today?

Test Answers:
Multiple Choice:
1. c
2. a
3. b
4. b
5. d
6. b
7. d
8. a
9. c
10. d
11. c
12. d
13. c

Essay Questions:
The following issues should be addressed in your answers:
1. Increased divorce rates;
   - Increased number of people living alone;
   - Increased number of couples remaining childless;
   - High rates of remarriage;
   - Alternative family forms.
2. Problems especially include poverty and single parenting;
   - Societal programs to better support impoverished families and parents who need to work and raise families. This especially gets into the issue of childcare facilities.
3. There are many issues to address. These could include any of the following:
   a. divorce legislation
   b. daycare and after-school programs
   c. provision of adequate income, housing, healthcare
   d. family counseling
   e. community and institutional supports for single parents
   f. greater child support from absent fathers
   g. more flexibility in the workplace.

CHAPTER THIRTEEN: PROBLEMS OF PUBLIC EDUCATION

Chapter Summary:
The chapter begins with an explanation of the importance placed on education in a democratic society. Sociological views, in the three main perspectives of education, are presented.
   Criticisms of the educational institutions in the U.S. are reviewed. These address issues of educational content; inequality in education; resistance to change in the institutions; teacher education and quality.
   Social policy issues are presented. These focus on the disparity between conservative and liberal viewpoints, preschool education programs, and open admissions to higher education.

Learning Objectives:
After studying the chapter the student should be able:
- to understand the philosophic views of education in the U.S.
- to explain the ways in which the three major sociological viewpoints explain education.
- to identify main areas of criticism leveled against education in the U.S.
- to elaborate social policy concerns in the field of education, particularly in terms of conservative versus liberal viewpoints.

Chapter Outline:
I. Public Education in the U.S.
   A. Education has been viewed as a means of maintaining democratic values and extending equality of opportunity.
   B. American schools have been criticized for failing to produce competent adults and for failing to eliminate social inequality. Different groups in society establish various goals for educational institutions.
II. Sociological Perspectives on Education
   A. Functionalists feel that people marginal to society cause problems in school. They also feel that some groups have values that deviate from societal norms.
   B. The conflict perspective looks at conflicts in the goals of education. Issues of bilingual education exemplify this view.
      1. Marxian views examine education as a mechanism for maintaining the status quo.
      2. Value conflict approach looks at the desire of particular groups to maintain their status.
   C. Interactionists look at various labels applied to

school children and their effects on achievement.
III. Education: An Institution Under Fire
   A. Education has been criticized for its failure to promote equal access. Inner-city minority students and rural minority students have been shown to receive inferior educations. Working class children also are educationally deprived as compared to white, middle-class students.
      1. Before WWI, 90% of blacks lived in the south and received inferior education in segregated settings. The lack of education among black parents has perpetuated educations differences along with segregation and discrimination.
      2. Educational attainment for Hispanics is also inferior. Language problems and de facto segregation hinder Hispanic education. Debates over the preservation of Hispanic culture and the need to assimilate into the mainstream continue today.
      3. Gaps in educational attainment have diminished somewhat but the dropout rate for Hispanics and blacks is still twice that of whites.
      4. Some argue that minority students suffer disadvantages at home, particularly because of low parental educational attainment.
      5. School dropouts are less likely to participate in the labor force and make less money when they do.
      6. Recent federal policy has cut the availability of funding for higher education.
   B. A 1983 commission report declared that the quality of education has fallen. Some support this assertion by pointing to declining SAT and achievement test scores. Some feel that these declines are not indicative of overall decline.
   C. Some theorists believe that schools are resistant to change. They believe that the bureaucratization of education has impeded change. They point to the number of specialists, hierarchy of authority, distance of policy makers from personnel who implement them, and relative teacher autonomy as evidence of resistance to change.
      1. New teaching materials, utilizing new technologies, often are not embraced by teachers or administrators.
   D. Desegregation occurred fairly rapidly in the southern and border states after the 1954 Supreme Court ruling. By the late 1960s, desegregation was hindered by de facto segregation and the policy of neighborhood school attendance. As a result, segregation today is greatest in the north.
   E. Teachers have demonstrated an increase in union

activity. By 1980, 30% of teachers belonged to the NEA or AFT. Unions have promoted increased salaries and status for teachers as well as educational policy demands. There appears to be an increased interest in teaching due to educational reforms, higher salaries for starting teachers, and projected teacher shortages.

IV. Social Policy

A. Conservative views in education promote a "back to basics" approach. This view stresses the role of education as a means to preserve culture and it promotes order, discipline, obedience. Its views were promoted by the findings of the 1983 report of the National Commission on Excellence in Education. It recommended focusing on: English, math, social studies, science, and computer science. It also recommended more rigorous academic standards. The commission was criticized for ignoring problems of teen unemployment, teacher burnout, high dropout rates, and special needs of the poor and minorities. It also ignored issues of decreased spending.

B. Liberal or humanistic views in education promote individual self-development and learning through experience. "Open-education" programs were promoted in the late 1960s and 1970s. There is little evidence to support their efficacy. The political climate of the 1980s supports conservative programs.

C. Preschool education has been supported as a means to advance the educational attainments of lower socioeconomic and minority students. The Perry Project indicated dramatic results from preschool education. These include: improved cognitive performance in early childhood; improved school performance; decreased delinquency, use of welfare, and teen pregnancy; increased high school graduation and college enrollment.

D. Higher education open admissions policies did increase overall educational opportunities in the City University of New York ("CUNY"). It doubled the number of blacks receiving degrees. However, ethnic segregation on its 17 campuses increased.

E. Some attention has been focused on teachers to improve education. These include merit (rather than seniority) raises; increased salaries; improved education courses; more rigid certification.

Key Terms:

SAT: Scholastic Aptitude Tests generally used in the process of admission to higher education.

de facto segregation: in schools, segregation stemming from segregation in neighborhoods.

NEA: National Education Association, a teachers' union.
AFT: American Federation of Teachers, a teachers' union.
Open Education: progressive programs emphasizing self-pacing, independence, and experiential learning.

Practice Test:
Multiple Choice Questions: Select the best answer for each of the questions below.
1. Which of the following statements is **NOT** true:
   a. education is considered essential to a democratic society
   b. by and large the schools have created equality
   c. parents in low socioeconomic statuses want their children to learn job-related skills
   d. teachers want parents to be more involved in education.
2. The highest per capita school expenditures are found in:
   a. the U.S.
   b. the USSR
   c. Japan
   d. Britain.
3. Which sociological perspective tends to see school problems as emanating from groups whose values differ from the overall society's:
   a. conflict
   b. Marxist
   c. functionalist
   d. labeling.
4. Which view tends to see the educational system as a means for maintaining the status quo:
   a. conflict
   b. interactionist
   c. functionalist
   d. labeling.
5. Which student is likely to receive the better education:
   a. rural whites
   b. inner-city blacks
   c. any Hispanic
   d. suburban working class.
6. Which of the following statements is **TRUE**:
   a. the educational gap between minorities and whites has widened since WWI.
   b. the black and Hispanic dropout rate is twice that of whites
   c. segregation in schools has been effectively wiped out
   d. the U.S. supports bilingual education all across the country.

7. Recent federal policy in higher education has:
   a. increased
   b. been completely cut
   c. cut loans
   d. cut grants.
8. Support for the argument that SAT score declines are significant include:
   a. the tests do not really measure educational institutions effectiveness
   b. they do not consider societal factors outside of educational institutions
   c. they reflect a similar drop in other cognitive test measures
   d. they fail to take into consideration changes in the tests.
9. Today the greatest school segregation is found in:
   a. the southwest
   b. the southeast
   c. the northeast
   d. the northwest.
10. Which of the following, regarding teachers, is **NOT** true:
    a. their union participation has decreased in the last twenty years
    b. starting salaries have improved
    c. there are projected shortages
    d. they have been more active in agitating for reforms.
11. The 1983 report from the Commission on Excellence in Education:
    a. promoted a back to basics curriculum
    b. addressed spending cuts
    c. aided in program policy for the poor
    d. addressed the problems of dropouts.
12. The Perry Preschool Project was dramatically effective in promoting educational attainment.
    a. true
    b. false.
13. Open admissions policies in New York's CUNY:
    a. increased the number of blacks receiving degrees
    b. decreased the number of blacks receiving degrees
    c. decreased ethnic segregation
    d. none of the above.

Essay Questions:
1. What do you think is the function of education in the U.S.?
2. Do you think full racial integration is desirable? Explain.
3. Do you support bilingual education? Why or why not?

Test Answers:
Multiple Choice Questions:
1. b
2. a
3. c
4. a
5. d
6. b
7. d
8. c
9. c
10. a
11. a
12. a
13. a

Essay Questions:
Students should address the following issues:
1. Teaching skills and information.
   - Social class maintenance and mobility.
   - Assimilation into the culture.
   - Producing people who will be compliant workers and conform to societal values.
   - The three perspectives in sociological theory should be addressed.
2. Issues of equal education and equal access to advancement should be addressed.
   - Feelings of inferiority should be addressed in terms of receiving a segregated educational experience.
   - The outcome of integrated schools is also important.
3. Address issues of maintaining some of the cultural heritage of minority groups.
   - Issues of promoting substantive learning before mastery of English.
   - Issues of assimilation into the mainstream culture.
   - Issues of conformity and achievement on the job.

CHAPTER FOURTEEN: CORPORATIONS, WORKERS, AND CONSUMERS

Chapter Summary:
The chapter begins with a discussion of the changing corporate structure in the U.S. Decreases in the number of corporations, increased multinational corporations, the global factory, and economic recessions are discussed. The effects of foreign competition and the demands of a service dominated structure are presented. Increased automation and the problems of displaced workers are also addressed. The repercussions of unemployment on the individual are also reviewed.

The nature of a consumer society is examined with special attention on the problems resulting from an economy based on credit. Advertising is an important element of consumer society. Social policy issues addressing the role of government in the economy and regulation of business is discussed as well as policy issues relating to employment.

Learning Objectives:
After studying the chapter the student should be able:
- to understand the nature of big business and the corporate structure today, particularly in relation to multinational corporations and the global factory, and the effects of these on the American worker.
- to explain the nature of the work experience in the U.S., with attention to the problems and causes of unemployment.
- to define the nature and problems associated with a consumer society.
- to explain social policy issues, particularly with regard to government intervention in business and to employment policies.

Chapter Outline:
I. Big Business and Corporate Power
   A. The U.S. exhibits a concentration of power in a few large corporations. Through expansion and merger, corporations have become complex organizations frequently run by salaried managers.
   B. Although the American marketplace has many products, their sources have actually decreased. Corporations have subsidiaries that produce materials and services related to the produce.
      1. The top 500 manufacturing corporations control sales and profits.
      2. Between 1954 and 1986, sales and net income of American corporations increased dramatically compared to the number of employees. This is largely due to automation and to the export of jobs and capital.

C. Corporate power in the U.S. has increased through mergers. Some feel these violate federal antitrust laws and disregard the needs of American workers. Many conglomerates engage in public relations campaigns to emphasize their benevolent contributions to society.
D. American multinational corporations outnumber those of any other nation. The influence of Japanese and European multinational firms has forced U.S. companies to adapt their products to local markets and to focus on long-term relations. Critics argue that multinational interests supersede those of the nation.
E. The global factory was made possible by: the ability to transport materials and products to anywhere in the world and by the ability to operate component operations anywhere in the world with cheap labor.
F. A decreasing number of employers dominate the labor market. Unions have become as large and centralized as the industries with which they deal. During the 1970s and 1980s, U.S. plants, factories, and mills have suffered lack of modernization and diversification while capital was diverted abroad. Older single industry cities and towns, many in the midwest, have suffered.
  1. Between 1979 and 1984, there were many displaced workers. In 1982, the UAW recommended wage and benefit reductions to its members to halt plant shutdowns. In some failing plants, workers have purchased the plants to own and operate them. Although there have been some successes in employee ownership the solution does not address the real problem.
G. Major corporations function to increase their income and profits. Subsidiaries to large corporations are justified by the trickle-down theory.

II. Work in Corporate America
A. The U.S. has experienced a shift from a manufacturing-based to a service-based economy. Four factors contribute to this:
  1. Since 1956, white collar workers have outnumbered blue collar workers. Within blue collar jobs, unskilled workers have decreased while skilled and semiskilled have increased.
  2. Increased specialization of jobs at all levels.
  3. Increases in low-wage jobs.
  4. Changes in the age and sex composition of the labor force.
B. Aspects of work that have been problematic include:
  1. Unemployment with its accompanying financial, social, and psychological features.
  2. Rise in chronic and intermittent unemployed.
  3. The discouraged or "invisibly" unemployed.
  4. Unemployed suffer from isolation and participate

less in community life.
   5. The underground economy causes the loss of tax revenues and fails to provide employee benefits to those involved in it.
   C. The next few decades will see more automation with, what many people feel, decreased number of jobs.
   1. Computer controlled automation will link together previously distinct aspects of production operations. Electronic data processing will perform increasing numbers of tasks formerly done by people. It will also automatically check the standards of many operators.
   2. Technology will cause many to feel that their boss is the computer. Work will become more demanding and, at the same time, reduce the opportunities for human interactions.
   D. Today's workers, raised in the affluence of the 1950s and 1960s, place more emphasis on individuality and independence. They are more interested in leisure and personal growth and less attached to particular companies.
   1. Today's workers feel a clash between their self-images and their jobs. Blue collar workers seem more dependent on the external satisfactions of the job.
   2. Many jobs are dull. Increased salaries can compensate for tedium or dangers at work.
   E. The American labor movement has focused on creating a safer and better work environment. Proponents of occupational health promote prevention of work-related diseases. Companies do not always act to ban unsafe materials unless officially labeled.
III. Consumers and Credit
   A. Much of the American economy depends upon the power of disposable income. Small businesses have been squeezed out by large corporations and franchise operations. Advertising is important and effects aspects of social life other than consumption patterns.
   B. Since the 1950s, the U.S. has been transformed into a credit society. This has given rise to the problem of debt entanglement.
IV. Social Policy
   A. Changes in the corporate power structure create issues in labor-management relations, government involvement in the economy, and planning versus laissez-faire approaches to the regulation of business.
   B. Special attention needs to be placed on the development of policies for displaced workers, and employment policies in general.

Key Terms:
Oligopolies: markets in which a small number of companies

or suppliers control a commodity or service.
Merger: the combining of separate businesses into a single enterprise.
Conglomerate: a combination of firms operating in many diverse fields.
Technostructure: key group of technicians who control the apparatus of production and have become the dominant economic force in society.
Multinational Corporations: economic enterprises headquartered in one country but with business activities in at least one other country.
Supranational Corporations: international corporations that operate across national boundaries.
Global Factory: companies no longer produce their products in just one country.
Outsourcing: locating plants that produce goods for the American market in third world nations.
Trickle-Down Theory: the notion that measures taken to aid business and wealthy individuals will stimulate economic activity and provide jobs and opportunities to the poor and unemployed.
White Collar Workers: professional, managerial, clerical, and sales personnel.
Underground Economy: the exchange of goods and services, legal or illegal, that is not monitored, recorded, or taxed by the government.
Flexitime: sliding work hours determined by the employee.
Consumer Society: an economy based on the activities of corporations depending on disposable income.

Practice Test:
Multiple Choice Questions: Select the best answer for each question below.
1. Which of the following statements is true:
   a. the available products in the U.S. have increased
   b. the corporations manufacturing products have in-increased
   c. subsidiaries do not have anything to do with the product of the parent company
   d. today there are 35 manufacturers of American automobiles.
2. Which of the following is NOT a reason for the decreased employment of the American worker:
   a. automation
   b. expert of manufacturing
   c. increased sales
   d. mergers of companies into new interests.
3. The U.S. labor market has suffered from multinational:
   a. increased investments in the U.S.
   b. outsourcing

c. changing policies at companies like Sony and Renault
   d. none of the above.
4. Research indicates displaced workers:
   a. are always reabsorbed by new industries
   b. are rarely reabsorbed by new industries
   c. will be reabsorbed a little more than 1/2 of the time
   d. none of the above.
5. In 1982, to deal with problems in American automobile manufacturing, the UAW recommended to its members:
   a. they get out of the industry
   b. they take cuts in pay and benefits
   c. they buy the plants
   d. they go on lay-off status.
6. The U.S. today is a(n) _____-based economy:
   a. agricultural
   b. manufacturing
   c. technological
   d. service.
7. Which of the following is NOT a basic feature of the American economy today:
   a. increased diversification of job skills
   b. increased women working
   c. increased low-wage jobs
   d. white collar jobs as the largest group.
8. Which group is considered to be newly added to the ranks of the unemployed:
   a. minorities
   b. women
   c. teens
   d. highly specialized white-collar workers.
9. Which of the following does NOT usually accompany unemployment:
   a. withdrawal from community life
   b. relief at getting a break from the tedium of work
   c. increased admissions to state mental hospitals
   d. loss of self-esteem.
10. Today's workers are considered to be:
    a. more interested in leisure and personal growth
    b. extremely loyal to particular companies
    c. interested in strictly enforced 9-5 days
    d. unresponsive to moves towards individuality and independence.
11. Blue-collar workers are MOST interested in:
    a. flexitime
    b. intrinsic rewards
    c. wages and vacations
    d. personal growth.
12. Many workers exposed to harmful materials:

a. quit
   b. file lawsuits against the companies
   c. stay from fear of unemployment
   d. none of the above.
13. Current social problems are often related to the base of today's economy in:
   a. cash
   b. credit
   c. barter
   d. services.

Essay Questions:
1. Explain the changing nature of the American workplace.
2. Explain the experiences of the unemployed in the U.S.
3. If you were in a position to do so, how would you modify the experience of work in the U.S.?

Test Answers:
Multiple Choice Questions:
1. a
2. c
3. b
4. c
5. b
6. d
7. a
8. d
9. b
10. a
11. c
12. c
13. b

Essay Questions:
Answers should address the following issues:
1. Issues addressed should include:
   - automation
   - multinational corporations
   - shrinking number of employees
   - foreign competition
   - economic recession
   - growing service sector
   - global factory.
2. Special attention should be placed on:
   - loss of income and financial support
   - social isolation
   - withdrawal from community activities
   - loss of self-esteem
   - obsolescence of skills.
3. Myriad issues addressed can be any of the following:
   - flexitime
   - greater worker control
   - shorter work week
   - greater employee benefits
   - job enrichment
   - job training.

CHAPTER FIFTEEN: URBAN PROBLEMS

Chapter Summary:
   The chapter begins with a historical overview of the growth of American cities. The U.S. traditionally has been characterized by an anti-urban bias. Theories explaining the consequences of urbanism are presented. The history of the development of transportation is correlated with urban developments.
   Cities manifest many problems with diverse repercussions. Some major problems are lack of adequate housing, federal budget cuts in aid to cities, deconcentration, the loss of manufacturing revenue, different family lifestyles, deteriorating infrastructures, and growing homelessness. The development of social policies to ameliorate these problems concludes the chapter.

Learning Objectives:
   After studying the chapter the student should be able:
   - to describe the history, definition, and attitudes towards American cities.
   - to explain the three theories of urbanism: Wirth's, compositionalism, subcultural theory.
   - to review the history of urban developments and the growth of the suburbs.
   - to identify and explain the problems that characterize cities.
   - to address social policy issues relating to urban life.

Chapter Outline:
I. The American City
    A. Urban growth was promoted by increasingly efficient transportation and communication, and the effects of industrialization. As cities grew so did social problems relating to them. Not until the twentieth century did medical and sanitary innovations make cities safe. The management of cities became more complicated by the mid-1850s due to the influx of immigrant populations. Political machines dominated and slums emerged.
    B. The American tradition contains a strong antiurban bias. Cities appear contrary to the "natural" relationship of the person and the environment. Cities have an image as "sinful."
    C. The majority of Americans live in major metropolitan areas. City populations are:
       1. Disproportionately minority, largely black. During the 1920s southern blacks migrated, to look for employment, to industrial cities in the northeast,

midwest, and south.
    2. There is much segregation in the cities, some voluntary but much involuntary.
    3. The elderly are also segregated in cities.

II. Theories of Urbanism

A. Louis Wirth argued that city life increased both social and personality disorders. He believed that in order to adapt to the intense stimuli of the city, people became withdrawn and isolated. He felt that bonds that united people were lost in city life. Loosening community ties created a sense of alienation. More freedom occurred with the cost of greater social and personal disruption.

B. Compositionalism asserts that the existence of small group interactions is perpetuated even in the urban setting. The strength of economic, cultural, and marital characteristics is felt to be more important than size or population density.

C. Subcultural theory maintains that people live within meaningful social worlds and urban life intensifies subcultures due to the large and diverse population within cities.

III. Metropolitan Growth

A. In the twentieth century the population flow has changed from rural/urban to intermetropolitan.

B. Transportation innovations have had a huge impact on the urban landscape. With the introduction of commuter railways, the suburbs became more viable. By the 1930s, the impact of the automobile heightened and dispersed the suburban growth.

C. Suburban growth has provided easier access to owning housing, has avoided the growth of public housing, encouraged industry to leave the city through the growth of highways, made the rehabilitation of central cities more difficult.

IV. Problems of Cities

A. Deconcentration of the cities has been progressing since the decade between 1920 and 1930. Migration out of central cities today is twice that of suburb to city movement. Recent years have seen a tremendous shift of the population to the sunbelt cities.

B. Manufacturing has relocated along the suburban highway systems. New specialized goods and services have moved into cities but the rate of growth in white collar work has been greater in suburban areas. Older manufacturing centers have been devastated by the expectation of manufacturing to developing nations and by the growth of high-tech industry.

C. Nontraditional family units flourish more readily in cities due to the lifestyle of cities. This has created

greater need for day care services, special programs, and welfare programs.
D. The real estate loss of central cities has damaged their tax base. The economic gap between suburbs and cities has worsened in recent years.
E. The cities infrastructures, often constructed in the late 1940s and 1950s, are in deteriorating conditions. There has been little federal aid forthcoming to aid in the rehabilitation of city bridges, roads, sewers, rail and water systems.

V. Shelter Poverty and Homelessness
A. One third of Americans are "shelter poor."
B. Poor, especially minority poor, are very likely to live in substandard housing. Urban removal projects drive the poor from their neighborhoods without providing adequate relocation.
C. Housing has become less affordable since 1980. Householders spend a larger portion of their income on rent. Growing numbers of people are homeless and cluster in large cities. Homeless people are a more diverse group than was previously true.

VI. Social Policy
A. The revitalization of central-city neighborhoods has been at the expense of the poor and the elderly. Revitalization must draw businesses back to the city to be successful. Programs are hampered by state and federal tax deficits and decreasing tax revenues.
B. The 1980s federal government reduced many programs providing housing assistance to citizens.

Key Terms:
Urbanism: a way of life dependent on heavy industry, mass communication, a mobile population, and mass consumer markets.
Agribusiness: large scale farming.
Urban Places: certain dense populations and manufacturing, commerce, administration, and specialized services.
Rural Areas: sparsely populated areas specializing in agriculture, forestry, and other exploitation of resources.
Urban Population: all persons in places with 2500 inhabitants or more that are incorporated as cities, villages, towns, boroughs.
Suburbs: closely settled incorporated or unincorporated places with 2500 inhabitants or more.
Urban Area or Conurbation: a city (or cities) with 50,000 or more inhabitants plus the surrounding suburbs.
Political Machines: local party organizations controlled by political "bosses" who distributed jobs and services.
Consolidated Metropolitan Statistical Area (CMSA): large metropolitan complexes with recognized subcenters that

have large core areas.
Primary Metropolitan Statistical Area (PMSA): large core areas within a CMSA.
Metropolitan Statistical Area (MSA): areas that have a large urban population nucleus and surrounding communities linked to it through social and economic activities.
Metropolitan Area: contains several urban communities.
Megalopolis: large metropolitan regions.
Outer Cities: large urban clusters on the perimeter of metropolitan areas.
Deconcentration: the erosion of the central city.
Infrastructure: physical facilities.
Gentrification: return of affluent people, often single and childless couples, to selected central city neighborhoods.
Shelter Poor: refers to the high cost of housing and the consequent lack of money for other necessities.

Practice Test:
Multiple Choice Questions: Select the best answer for each question below.
1. Which of the following regarding urbanization is **NOT** true:
    a. the lines between urban and rural are blurred
    b. population density distinguished rural and urban
    c. the suburbs have decreased significantly in the past twenty years
    d. small farms have given way to agribusiness.
2. Modern sanitation developed to aid the health conditions of the city:
    a. during colonial times
    b. after the Revolutionary War
    c. after the Civil War
    d. in the early twentieth century.
3. Residential segregation of blacks in cities:
    a. no longer occurs much
    b. is largely voluntary
    c. is largely involuntary
    d. does not limit lifestyle choices.
4. Wirth's theory of urbanism asserts:
    a. the maintenance of primary group ties even in cities
    b. increased social and personality disorders
    c. lack of societal restraint and personal emotional support
    d. increased personal freedoms.
5. Which is considered to be bigger:
    a. urban centers
    b. metropolitan centers
    c. megalopolis
    d. cities.
6. Which of the following has **NOT** been a consequence of

suburbanization:
a. the loss of industry to nearby suburbs along the highways
b. the easier renovation of central cities
c. the concentration of public housing in cities
d. the tendency for homeowners to be concentrated outside cities in suburbs.

7. Which of the following is **NOT** a contributor to deconcentration:
a. suburban flight
b. the influx of poor minority groups
c. the daily flow into the city of nonresidents
d. the abundance of skilled labor jobs in central cities.

8. Migration within the U.S. in recent years has been largely:
a. back to industrial cities
b. to sunbelt cities
c. to rural communities
d. to the southeast.

9. Which of the following is **NOT** true of urban renewal projects:
a. they facilitate gentrification
b. they remove slum housing
c. they settle original residents into the redevelopments
d. they restrict federal public housing only to the very poor.

10. Which of the following regarding central cities is **NOT** true:
a. continue to show unequivocal decay
b. are regaining some of the lost business of previous decades
c. still attract the affluent to expensive high-rise apartments
d. have, in some cities, been revitalized.

Essay Questions:
1. Which theory of urbanism seems most accurate to you?
2. What do you think are the most serious problems facing cities today?
3. How would you tackle problems of the cities?

Test Answers:
Multiple Choice Questions:
1. c
2. d
3. c
4. a
5. c
6. b
7. d
8. b
9. c
10. a

Essay Questions:
Answers should address the following issues:
1. This is largely a matter of opinion but Wirth's assertion of social and personality disorders should be addressed. Many people enjoy cities, are they all anomic? Contrast to compositional approach. Issues of subcultural affiliation should also be addressed.
2. Any of the following:
    - lack of tax revenues
    - gentrification
    - lack of housing for poor and low-income
    - poor infrastructure
    - lack of jobs
    - deconcentration.
2. Any of the following:
    - housing policy in federal government
    - federal aid and policy
    - Restructuring municipal/suburban finance structures
    - grant incentives for manufacturing and business to move back to cities, create jobs, and boost economy.

CHAPTER SIXTEEN: POPULATION AND IMMIGRATION

Chapter Summary:

The chapter begins with a review of the status of the current world population. Increases in population are due largely to improvements in public health measures. Decreases in fertility also contribute to declining population size.

The U.S. population is undergoing an increase in population due to the large number of people in reproductive years.

Various measures to control the population size include reducing growth rates, stabilizing population size, or achieving a negative growth rate.

The U.S. has a long history of supporting immigration. In the 1990s, immigration is expected to average 700,000 people annually. Immigration is a big aspect of social policy as absorbing the costs of immigration has consequences for many different societal groups.

Learning Objectives:

After studying the chapter, the student should be able:
- to discuss the history and current status of world population trends.
- to explain the changing composition and demographics of the U.S. population.
- to elaborate the three approaches to population control.
- to explain the various issues surrounding immigration policy in the U.S.

Chapter Outline:

I. The World Population
   A. The world population was 5 billion in 1987 and, if it grows at the current rate, it will double in 45 years.
   B. Increases in the population are due to longevity increases. These are a result of improved sanitation, disease control, and public health.
   C. Demographic transitions characterize industrialized nations.
   D. Annual immigration, to the U.S., in the 1990s is expected to be over 700,000.
   E. Decreases in fertility may be attributed to declining marriages, increased birth control and abortions, and reductions in desired family size.
   F. Rising expectations refers to the belief that improved conditions will be extended to a larger portion of the population.

II. The U.S. Population
   A. Present population growth is due to the number of people of childbearing age. The proportion of growth among older ethnic groups is falling while those of new ethnic groups is increasing.
III. Population Control
   A. There are three approaches:
      1. reduce the rate of growth;
      2. stabilize the size;
      3. achieve a negative rate of growth.
   B. Sterilization and limiting family size are strategies to reduce population size in less developed countries.
IV. Immigration and its Consequences
   A. U.S. immigration can be divided into five periods:
      1. Early Colonial - to 1790;
      2. Old Northwest European - 1820 to 1885;
      3. Southern and Eastern Europe - 1885 to 1940;
      4. Post-World War II Refugee - 1945 to 1968;
      5. The New Immigration - 1968 to the present.
   B. By 1990, one in four Americans were of African, Asian, Hispanic, or Native American descent.
   C. The federal government does not provide financial support to cities taking a disproportionately high number of immigrants.
   D. Much illegal immigration to the U.S. occurs. Every year 1.2 million such people are located by the U.S. Immigration Service.
V. Social Policy
   A. Social policy today in the U.S. focuses on immigration policy. Support for immigration is found among employers of immigrant labor. Some Americans are working to eliminate all civil rights related restrictions on immigration.

Key Terms:
Crude Birthrate: the number of births per 1000 population.
Rate of population Growth (or "natural increase"): the differential between the crude birthrate and the death rate.
Demographic Transition: population shifts from an equilibrium in death and birthrates to low death and birthrates in a larger population.
Total Fertility Rate: average number of children born to women throughout the childbearing years.
Zero Population Growth: end population growth by lowering birthrates.
Family Planning: helping individuals control their fertility.

Population Control: addressing population concerns at the societal level.
Nativism: anti-immigration or anti-foreigner sentiments.
Principle of Family Unification: priority is given to immigrants with close relatives in the U.S.
Marielitos: former political prisoners from Cuba.
Chain Migration: the tendency of immigrants to migrate to areas with relatives or people from their home countries.
Coyotes: smugglers aiding Latin American illegal immigrants.

Practice Test:
Multiple Choice Questions: Select the best answer for each question below.
1. The world population is currently:
   a. doubling every ten years.
   b. decreasing rapidly.
   c. decreasing in a few European and Scandinavian countries.
   d. remaining stable.
2. Demographic transitions are:
   a. complete in all nations.
   b. in their third stage in industrialized nations.
   c. absent in developing nations.
   d. no longer a factor in population changes.
3. The country with the largest per capita consumption of energy is:
   a. the U.S.S.R.
   b. China
   c. India
   d. the U.S.
4. New ethnic groups include:
   a. Irish
   b. Italians
   c. Hispanics
   d. Jews
5. Which country has actually adapted policies to increase family size?
   a. France
   b. the U.S.
   c. Australia
   d. South Africa
6. The first laws establishing immigration quotas and controls were passed in:
   a. 1885
   b. 1901
   c. 1921
   d. 1946
7. Today's immigrants come largely from:
   a. the U.S.S.R.

b. India
   c. Europe
   d. Latin America
8. By 1990, one in _____ Americans were of African, Asian, Hispanic, or Native American ancestry.
   a. two
   b. four
   c. five
   d. seven
9. Illegal immigrants identified each year are about:
   a. 200,000
   b. 700,000
   c. 1.2 million
   d. 5 million
10. Which group is no longer excluded from immigrating?
    a. people with infectious disease.
    b. homosexuals.
    c. people with no skills and no relatives.
    d. people with certain political beliefs.

Essay Questions:
1. What is the significance of changes in the composition of the U.S. population?
2. What are some of the significant issues in addressing U.S. immigration policy?

Test Answers:
Multiple Choice Questions:
1. c
2. b
3. d
4. c
5. a
6. c
7. d
8. b
9. c
10. b

Essay Questions:
Students should address the following issues:
1. -Baby boom babies are of childbearing age.
   -Ethnic composition is changing due to immigration.
   -New ethnic groups tend to have significantly younger average ages.
2. -Job competition.
   -Maintenance of cheap labor.
   -Disproportionate burdens of immigrants in particular cities.
   -No federal government aid to cities with high numbers of immigrants.

CHAPTER SEVENTEEN: TECHNOLOGY AND THE ENVIRONMENT

Chapter Summary:
The chapter defines technology as all the apparatus, activities, and organizational networks associated with technology. Technological changes are viewed in the context of their consequences. These include social, economic, and environmental impacts. Environmental concerns include water and air pollution, toxic waste, waste disposal, disturbance of the ecological system, and energy sources and production.

The U.S. consumes a disproportionate amount of the world's energy. Future social policy needs to take consideration of all the aspects of technological change, especially environmental and world impact.

Learning Objectives:
After studying the chapter, the student should be able:
- to define technology.
- to explain the far reaching consequences (social, economic, and environmental) of technological changes.
- to elaborate attitudes and concerns about technology.
- to describe the impact of technology of the natural environment.
- to analyze the impact of technology in terms of environmental stress.
- to explain U.S. relation to the world environment.
- to identify social policy issues arising from technology.

Chapter Outline:
I. Defining Technology
   A. In the broadest sense, technology includes all the apparatus, activities, and organizational networks associated with it.
II. Technological Dualism
   A. Technological innovation causes drastic and extremely rapid changes in the work available to Americans.
III. Controlling Technology
   A. In the 1980s, the U.S. economy created new jobs but automation reduced the number of new jobs in manufacturing.
   B. Two fears about technology held by some are:
      1. harm to people and the environment.
      2. the inability to completely control technology.
IV. Technology and Institutions
   A. Cultural lag occurs when two parts of the culture are modified so that less adjustment exists between them than previously.
V. Technology and the Natural Environment

    A. Two developments -- accelerated technological and scientific change and rapid population growth -- are causing pollution and depletion of the natural environment.
    B. Sometimes seemingly benign technologies have unanticipated consequences.
VI. Environmental Stress
    A. Best understood as the interaction of three systems: the natural environment, the technological system, and the social system.
    B. Air pollution comes from organic compounds; lead and other metals; particulate matters; motor vehicles; manufacturing processes.
    C. Water pollution is apparent in all phases of the hydrologic cycle.
    D. Two principal methods of solid waste disposal include landfills and incineration.
VII. The U.S. and the World Environment
    A. The U.S. is the wealthiest and most polluting nation. The U.S. consumes one-third of the world's energy.
VIII. Social Policy
    A. Policy issues include consideration of controlling new technology, assessing technological impact, considering the relative value of technological change and environmental consequences, the need for public education.

Key Terms:
Technological Change: refers to change in any of the major dimensions associated with technology.
Cultural Lag: when social change is not as rapid as technological change.
Automation: the replacement of workers by a nonhuman means of producing the same product.
Technological Determinism: the idea that technological innovation dictates changes in social institutions and culture.
Environmental Stress: refers to concepts including interdependence, diversity, limits, and complexity.
Acid Rain: the large concentrations of sulfur dioxide in rainfall.
Biologic Magnification: refers to increases in the concentration of substances as they ascend the food chain.
Postindustrial Society: societies dominated by theoretical knowledge.
Futurists: heterogeneous group of social analysts who try to describe and plan for the future.

Practice Test:
Multiple Choice Questions: Select the best answer for each question below.
1. "Technological have-nots" would include:
   a. inner city ghettos
   b. remote rural areas
   c. people in less developed nations
   d. all of the above.
2. What technological change has contributed to the _exportation_ of manufacturing jobs?
   a. jet planes
   b. satellite communication
   c. automation
   d. cultural lag
3. The _Challenger_ explosion is an example of:
   a. technology out of control
   b. failure to identify problems in the technology
   c. the ineffectiveness of some whistle blowing
   d. the high value placed on safety at all cost.
4. Energy through fusion:
   a. supplies 20% of the U.S. energy
   b. is completely safe
   c. probably is not as economical as solar energy
   d. is an alternative accepted by nearly every U.S. citizen.
5. The "cold fusion" experiment reported in the late 1980s:
   a. was never replicated
   b. demonstrates sound scientific methodology
   c. paved the way for great changes in energy technology.
   d. none of the above.
6. Which of the following has been found to be harmful to animal and/or human life?
   a. pesticides
   b. aerosol cans
   c. herbicides
   d. all of the above.
7. Environmental stress:
   a. refers to pollution
   b. includes concepts of interdependence, diversity, limits, and complexity.
   c. is not relevant to understanding technology
   d. is a simple concept with one dimension
8. Ecological consequences of pollution include:
   a. acid rain
   b. breakdown of the ozone
   c. global warming
   d. all of the above
9. The Chernobyl accident:
   a. created high levels of radioactive gases
   b. had little ecological consequences

    c. created no dangers for humans
    d. had only short-term consequences
10. Proponents of appropriate technology:
    a. desire a return to preindustrial lifestyles
    b. oppose large scale technologies
    c. are against the development of solar and wind energy
    d. none of the above

Essay Questions:
1. Discuss the notion that technological innovation is progress.
2. What are social policy issues associated with technology and its environmental impact?

Test Answers:
Multiple Choice Questions:
1. d
2. b
3. c
4. c
5. a
6. d
7. b
8. d
9. a
10. b

Essay Questions:
Students should address the following issues:
1. -Environmental impact.
   -Social consequences.
   -Economic consequences.
   -Quality of life.
   -Necessity of the new technology in question.
2. -Ecological impact.
   -Who will regulate the technology.
   -Who/what will be effected.
   -Protection of citizen's safety.
   -Quality of life.

CHAPTER EIGHTEEN: WAR AND TERRORISM

Chapter Summary:

War entails various consequences for nations both as a direct result of the warfare as well as in indirect consequences such as the diversion of resources. Today's nuclear weapons have the power to destroy the world as we know it.

Theories about warfare are diverse, ranging from genetic explanations to ones rooted in political-economics. Terrorism is an increasingly prevalent form of warfare. Social policy needs to address mechanisms for responding to terrorist activity and for reducing the threat of nuclear war.

Learning Objectives:

After studying the chapter, the student should be able:
- to identify the history and present status of warfare.
- to elaborate the consequences of war.
- discuss the technology and organization of war.
- explain the basic theoretical views of warfare.
- to explain the nature of terrorism.
- to identify issues needed to be addressed at the social policy level.

Chapter Outline:
I. The Nature of the Problem
   A. Direct effects of war include death, injury, and property damage. The poor suffer a disproportionate amount of personal injuries in the military.
   B. Indirect effects of war include mass migrations of the population, economic damage, impact on thought in the culture.
   C. The capacity of nuclear war to annihilate the human species cannot be overstated. Today's bombs are 1600 times more powerful than the one that destroyed Hiroshima.
II. Military Technology and the Conduct of War
   A. Changes in the organizational dimension of military technology have been as important as advances in military apparatus.
III. Theories About War and Its Origins
   A. Ethological and sociobiological theories hold that aggression enhanced the species capacity for survival and so became encoded into the genes.
   B. Clausewitz's theory of war views war as a means to an end, engaged in when the benefits outweigh the costs.
   C. The Marxist view of war is one in which the interests of the bourgeoisie are served in warfare.
   D. Debate exists over the issue of whether a strong

military encourages or deters warfare.
   E. International forces promoting peace include cooperative organizations, such as the U.N., and international trade.
IV. Terrorism: Undeclared War
   A. Terrorism is often used by a nation, or by a political movement within a nation, to call attention to its cause.
V. Social Policy
   A. There has been progress in limiting conventional weapons and increased hope of reducing the likelihood of nuclear war.
   B. The major powers have formulated treaties to limit certain weapons and regulate the spread of others.
   C. The SALT treaties were efforts at arms control between the U.S. and the Soviet Union.
   D. Some feel the best deterrent to the arms race would come from public pressure.
   E. Official policies insist on noncompliance with terrorists.

Key Terms:
Post-Traumatic Stress Disorder (PTSD): irritability and depression following war experiences, often accompanied by nightmares and flashbacks.
Hiroshima: the site, in Japan, of the first explosion of a nuclear weapon during a war.
Jus ad bellum: justification for going to war.
Jus in bello: justifiable acts in wartime.
The Power Elite: a book in which C.W. Mills asserts that military leaders are more powerful than ever before in U.S. history.
Nationalism: the identification of the masses with the idea of nationhood and the exaltation of the nation's culture.
Terrorism: the use of warlike tactics against nonmilitary populations.
Transnational Terrorism: violent acts carried out by essentially autonomous independent agents.
Arms Control: permitting certain levels of particular weapons.
Arms Prohibition: banning entirely particular weapons.

Practice Test:
Multiple Choice Questions: Select the best answer for each question below.
1. Which period has been the deadliest in human history?
   a. the cavemen period
   b. the Middle ages
   c. the Colonial period

d. the twentieth century
2. The first nuclear bomb used in war:
   a. has not yet occurred
   b. was dropped on Hiroshima in 1945
   c. was used during the Vietnam War in the 1960s
   d. was followed rapidly by several other countries
3. Which of the following is true with regard to <u>jus in bello</u>?
   a. the rules are difficult to enforce
   b. the rules are frequently violated
   c. civilians often are killed
   d. all of the above
4. Ethological theories of war rely on _____ explanations.
   a. cultural
   b. biological
   c. psychological
   d. political
5. In the Marxist view, World War I was:
   a. a randomly timed act of warfare
   b. the product only of specific events leading up to it
   c. a search for new colonies
   d. none of the above
6. Terrorism is likely to be viewed as:
   a. an outright act of war
   b. a covert act of intimidation
   c. a completely legitimate means of making a point
   d. an internationally sanctioned mode of conflict resolution
7. Which of the following is **NOT** typically a target of terrorist attacks?
   a. prominent persons
   b. random victims
   c. people in business
   d. children
8. The "cold" war refers to the 45 years of antagonism between:
   a. Cambodia and Vietnam
   b. China and Japan
   c. the U.S. and the U.S.S.R.
   d. Ireland and England
9. The SALT treaties failed to:
   a. stop the development of new weapons
   b. include the Soviet Union
   c. prevent the development of new weapons
   d. achieve compliance

<u>Essay Question</u>:
1. What issues relating to war need to be addressed at the social level?

Test Answers:
Multiple Choice Questions:
1. d
2. b
3. d
4. b
5. c
6. b
7. d
8. c
9. a

Essay Questions:
Students should address the following issues:
1. -Arms control.
   -Arms freeze.
   -SALT.
   -Popular sentiment.
   -Threats from nonsuper power states.
   -International politics.